WITCH CITY DETECTIVE

A Salem Police Detective's Journey through the 70s, 80s, and 90s

JAMES R. GAUTHIER

James R. Gauthier
410 Salem Street #403
Wakefield, MA 01880

First Edition, 2024

ISBN: 979-8-9904148-1-5 (paperback)

Self-Published by James R. Gauthier

CONTENTS

PREFACE

As I sit down to pen this book, the memories of my career as a police officer and Detective in Salem, Massachusetts, come rushing back, not as mere recollections but as vivid chapters of a life lived in the service of others. This book, woven from years of sacrifice and dedication, is more than a personal endeavor. It's a tribute to the profession of law enforcement that demanded everything of me and several others, often at the cost of precious family time.

The catalyst for this book was my son, Mike, and my family at large, who encouraged me to put my many stories in writing. His words, "Dad, your stories are too good to be forgotten, and others need to hear them," echoed in my mind, turning a mere thought into a reality. I can remember many summers driving around Salem with my family and friends, telling stories of houses we raided, cases we solved, and high-speed chases experienced. It was time to put these stories in writing.

Salem, a city as mysterious as it is historic, has been the backdrop of my career. The cases that I encountered, ranging from the mundane to the extraordinary, are not just tales of crime and justice. They are reflections of humanity, each case a complex web of emotions, decisions, and consequences. Sharing these stories is not just about preserving the past; it's about offering insights into a city and its some of its people during a timeframe that many people have forgotten.

Above all, this book is an ode to the sacrifices inherent in police work. The long hours away from family, the missed birthdays and anniversaries were the unspoken cost of wearing the badge. This book is a testament to the sacrifices that all police officers endure. It is also a reminder that behind every case, every uniform, is a human being with a family, a heart, and a story to tell.

In these pages, you will find more than just a chronicle of cases from Salem. You will find the heart of police Detectives and me, who served passionately, and the spirit of a unique city. Welcome to a journey through the eyes of a Salem Police Detective.

Certain names of individuals presented in this book have been altered to safeguard their privacy. This measure has been meticulously taken to ensure that while the essence and integrity of the stories remain intact, the identities of those involved are also protected.

∼

"Service to others is the rent that we pay for our room here on earth."

-MUHAMMAD ALI

THE
WILLOWS
AREA

THE PANTHER

Location: *149 Derby Street (Rear)*

Coordinates: *42.52171*N, 70.88589*W*

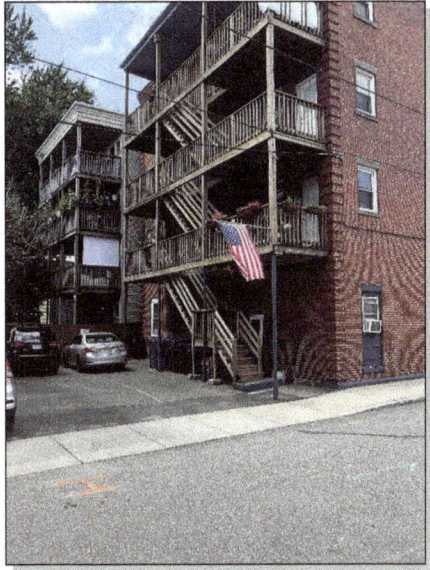

In 1990, we had a case where we got called down to Derby Street to a small apartment across from the "In a Pig's Eye" restaurant. The report was that a college student was sexually assaulted. When we arrived on the scene, the woman was in hysterics. We calmed her down, and she started telling us what had happened. Apparently, she was out food shopping. As she was unloading her car to bring the groceries inside her apartment, a man came running up to her, out of breath. He asked her if he could use a telephone. This was the time before cell phones were predominant. The guy said he was a private detective and had to get in touch with his partner. He also said his radio was not working, and his car broke down. Unfortunately, she fell for the story and let him in. As soon as he first stepped into the apartment, he grabbed her, put his hand over her mouth, and tied her up. He gagged her with a sock in her mouth and assaulted her violently. He then left her.

We got the call just after the incident, and she gave us a description of a man with a reddish face. He smelled of alcohol a little bit, and she described him as having a tattoo in an unusual place. It was a tattoo of a panther, tearing through the man's skin and leaping directly out of his thigh with its head between its paws. The woman ended up giving us a composite, which was done the old-fashioned way. It was put together with clear overlays, like the shape of a face, the shape of a mustache, and then the eyes. We then put the whole composite together and laid it on the copy machine glass. The look of the face came out on the copy.

We got right on the case and interviewed a bunch of people that we thought might be involved in this thing. It all turned up with negative results. This was before DNA was mainstream in law enforcement, so every time we arrested anybody or had someone in custody, we checked to see if they had any sort of panther tattoo on the right thigh. Whenever we got something close, we contacted the victim and asked if that was the tattoo. She said no to each one, as she knew exactly what she saw.

Almost a year to the day of the assault had passed, the victim came to the police station with a yearbook from Salem State College. In the yearbook was a group photo of a bunch of students who were sleeping outside to show support for the homeless people in the area. In this photo was a man that the victim said looked exactly like her assailant. Through some more investigation, we found out who that individual was and had him come down to the police station for questioning. I proceeded to interview him and told him that we were investigating an assault case. Next, I said that one thing about the person we were looking for was that he had a tattoo in an usual spot. The next thing this suspect said shocked me!

"Well, I've got a tattoo in a different part of my body," he said.

"Oh…well, where is it?" I replied.

"It's on my upper leg but towards the side of my rear end. It's sort of on my thigh," he responded.

Immediately, I said, "You have the right to remain silent…" et cetera, et cetera—the Miranda Rights.

"I did not do anything!" he pleaded.

"Well, can I see your tattoo?" I said.

So, he pulled his drawers down and showed me his tattoo. It was of rainbows, clouds, unicorns, and birds flying. I said to myself, oh my goodness! I did not expect that. If this was the guy who assaulted the victim, maybe he had the panther tattoo strategically covered up. I found out where he received his tattoo that he showed me. It was a parlor in New

Hampshire. Another officer and I took a trip up over the border to the tattoo shop. The artist confirmed that he inked the guy with clouds and unicorns, and he confirmed that nothing was underneath prior. He did not cover up another tattoo. That negated him as a suspect, and we disregarded him at that point, even though he did look an awful lot like the composite.

Over the years, time had passed, and we contacted the victim to check in whenever something came up. During those days, Massachusetts law had a statute of limitations of 15 years for sexual assault. It was getting very close to the 15 years that this case would be unable to be prosecuted. Jim Page, a Detective I was working with at the time, had attended a class on the new advancements in DNA testing. He came back from that training, and we talked about it in the office. I told him that maybe we should see if we can get a match on any DNA samples from the victim's case. We requested a test be run with the MA State Police crime lab.

Lo and behold, a couple of weeks later, we got a call from the State Police that they had a match for a guy who was locked up for murder in the prison system. We found out that this guy's name was Tim Crenshaw. We investigated his background and discovered that he was infamous for assaulting females. We learned that he was arrested in Revere for a sexual assault. He also traveled down to Fort Lauderdale, Florida, where he worked at a fancy restaurant as a waiter. One night, he was at the Holiday Inn down in Fort Lauderdale on Route 1 and met a couple of young ladies at the bar. One of the ladies decided to go to her room to make herself a cocktail because the drinks were expensive. Crenshaw followed her up there and violently sexually assaulted her. The woman gave a description of the individual to the police later that night.

The police down there ended up finding and arresting him immediately. They asked the girls if they would testify against him in court. However, they were on a trip, traveling from one country to another and throughout different parts of the US. She was very hesitant about testifying because they were in the middle of this worldwide trip. They just wanted to get onto the rest of their lives. So, they let Crenshaw go.

After we got our DNA tests back, we got in touch with the MA Dept of Corrections and got descriptions of Crenshaw's tattoos. Sure enough, one of the tattoos that he had inked was that of a leaping panther on his right thigh. We got a picture of that, and I jumped on the phone with the victim.

"Hello, this is Jim Gauthier," I said.

"You must be calling to tell me one of two things. You're retiring, or you caught him," she replied.

"Well, it's both. I am retiring, and yes, we finally caught him."

I ended up telling her who it was and showed her the photograph of the panther, which she perfectly described. Crenshaw was going to be arraigned on charges, even though he was already serving a life sentence for killing a 14-year-old girl. Our victim wanted to go forward with the charges mainly to finish that chapter in her life.

To close this story out, we ended up going to court, and Crenshaw was planning to plead guilty. However, when he walked into the courtroom, he saw some court reporters and a couple of cameras. Due to the attention and coverage, he reneged on his promise to plead guilty.

"I'm not doing this in front of all these people. There was not supposed to be anybody here," Crenshaw said. Crenshaw turned around, and the court officer escorted him back to the prison transport vehicle. Our victim was very upset. Her husband at the time and her family were also very upset. Detective Page and I were as well. Page and I said to each other that if we were going to trial with Crenshaw present, we were going to have to subpoena some of Crenshaw's relatives to add pressure. We subpoenaed his sister, who was living over in Swampscott, his mother, and his stepfather too. We told them they would have to come to court to testify. Apparently, the sister did not want anything to do with her brother. She did not want any affiliation in any way as he was a convicted murderer. She was living in a kind of affluent neighborhood, so she did not want her name to be associated with him at all. It would have tarnished her reputation.

The sister's husband ended up visiting Crenshaw in jail and explained the situation to him that Salem PD was using subpoena powers to make this happen. He said to Crenshaw that if you did this, that he should "man up," talk, and confess to it. He said the sisters and the family are mortified that they'd have to come in and testify. That visit worked because Crenshaw had a change of heart. A couple of weeks later, he came into Superior Court and admitted to sexually assaulting our victim.

That was the end of a long chapter for us and the victim. She knew that the person who did this to her was off the street and wouldn't be hurting anybody else in the future.

SUMMER BASH OUT OF CONTROL

Location: *Cheval and Beach Avenue*

Coordinates: *42.53366*N, 70.86591*W*

Back in the '70s, there was a lot of strife and social unrest within the country. The Salem Police Department at that time decided that it would be a strategic move to form and train a tactical police unit to disperse crowds and handle riot type situations. Back then, this was considered progressive. There was a police officer out of Boston PD, named Arthur Lamb, who developed training and a curriculum on the usage of police batons. The curriculum covered awareness, stance work, grip, striking combinations, and approaches to riot control. The baton that we used back then would be held in the palm of the hand and the rest of the club would lean along the bottom of the forearm. There was a protruding end to the club for jabs and thrusts to the front. It was essentially a police version of a tonfa stick that martial artists used to use in the '70s.

There were probably 25 or 30 police officers that started doing this training. There was a new garage downtown that we used as the training facility. The training was pretty cool. We learned how to handle and use the club in various situations and then how to get into a formation for riot control situations. It was a "V" type formation like the tip of a spear. Once the formation was made, and the baton was in a certain position, we would shuffle step forward with a thrust, then shuffle back. At the same time, we all let out a grunting sound at the same time. It was like a psychological effect on the receiving party.

So on to the story. Every year down the Willows area behind the amusement park / arcade, the neighborhood always threw a block party. It could have been for the 4th of July or just a regular block party I do not quite remember. However, the organizers strictly monitored their own crowd with regards to keeping "outsiders" out. This particular year, probably 1976, or '77 the crowd got a little bit boisterous, and some outside individuals had infiltrated. Neighbors that lived down there called the organizers of the party and started complaining about people urinating on their lawns, getting rowdy, and throwing beer cans all over the ground. The place was getting trashed.

The party really started to get out of control, and the neighborhood group couldn't handle the situation any further. The call then went out to Salem Police to help quell the situation. This newly formed riot management team quickly mobilized, got into our cruisers, and went down to the area. We parked at the end of Columbus Avenue, got out of the vehicles, and got into formation. We formed the "V" and started our shuffle step towards the mass of people that were down there!

The people were taken aback when they saw us, because this would be something that you would see in large city type riots. This was just a lower scale kind of situation. However, we took it seriously, nonetheless. All of us also knew that we would probably run into some people (figuratively and literally) that we knew. Our thought was that because we knew them, that they would hopefully just disperse on their own.

Wearing our 1970s riot helmets, shuffling, and grunting away all together we moved right through the crowd. It did not take long for things to settle down. We discovered that the neighborhood people knew who the outsiders were. They ended up pointing out different people to us that shouldn't have belonged there. We scooted those people away, and I do not recall making arrests.

The "V" formation with the Lamb method did squash the situation, but it was the first and last time that we used it. It was a little too aggressive. Sometimes just some simple de-escalation tactics work just as well. The only other times that things even came close to that type of mass of unruly people were the crowds towards the end of the Halloween night. Back then though, we had the luxury of the Boston Police Mounted Patrol Units come down and disperse everyone at the end of the night.

NORTH SALEM AREA

HARMONY GROVE INCIDENT

Location: *Harmony Grove Cemetery – Caretaker's House*
Coordinates: *42.52422*N, 70.91124*W*

It was a spring day, and Officer Jim Page (a future fellow Detective) got called to Harmony Grove Cemetery for a person having difficulty breathing. A caretaker and his family lived onsite at the time, and someone had called the police department to report a breathing issue with a family member. When Jim arrived, he went up to the second floor of the caretaker's house and found an individual lying on his stomach in the bedroom with a shotgun lying underneath him. The person had taken his own life via a shotgun blast.

This victim, I remember, was kind of a survivalist. He had crossbows, knives, and all sorts of stuff in his bedroom closet. People who take their own life will typically leave a note or something to give some insight into what their life was like and why they did it. In this case, the victim had a little ceramic plate on his bed beside where he was lying on the floor, saying, "The Dead-End Kid." That was his short epitaph / going away message. He was the "Dead-End Kid." As it turned out, he ended his own life with a shotgun and made quite a mess in this room. I came onto the scene later to assist Jim.

An interesting personal coincidence that I felt was book-worthy was that I knew this room of the house! Several years prior, I dated the caretaker's daughter, and the room where this incident happened was the daughter's room! Very strange coincidence, I thought at the time.

An autopsy of the victim was performed at the Boston City Hospital out of protocol. The Boston City Hospital's autopsy room was like an archaic, medieval castle-type atmosphere. I mean, big stone columns from top to bottom, stone walls, and it was old-looking. Another Detective who was just promoted to the Criminal Investigation Division (CID) at the Salem Police Department, Conrad Prosniewski, went with me to this autopsy. It was Conrad's very first experience. A shotgun blast does severe damage to a person's body, and looking at the aftermath in this setting was odd, eerie, and unnatural. It was like a scene from a horror movie.

I'll say it throughout this book and explain why in further chapters and stories, but a little bit of humor comes with tragedy in this profession. It was part of a coping mechanism that we, as law enforcement officers, employed to overcome very difficult situations. This was also similar in the military, where soldiers like me used this tactic while in combat. Anyway, we arrived at the autopsy room downstairs in the basement. There was a big stone pillar that I remember Conrad putting his back up against it, and he said, "I don't want to look. I don't want to look." The situation made him a bit freaked out. However, this reaction was completely normal. Anyone's first viewing of severe trauma would react like that and the same thing happened to me at my first one. I remember saying something like, "Come on, Conrad, toughen up," jokingly. At this point, the body is just a piece of something laying on the table that used to be a human being. Police officers, at some point, make that distinction after desensitization to situations like this. Conrad and I went through the autopsy, and it was obvious what the cause of death was.

THE CALVIN DANIELS CASE

Location: *Various, Harmony Grove Road*

Coordinates: *Various, 45.52418*N, 70.91670*W*

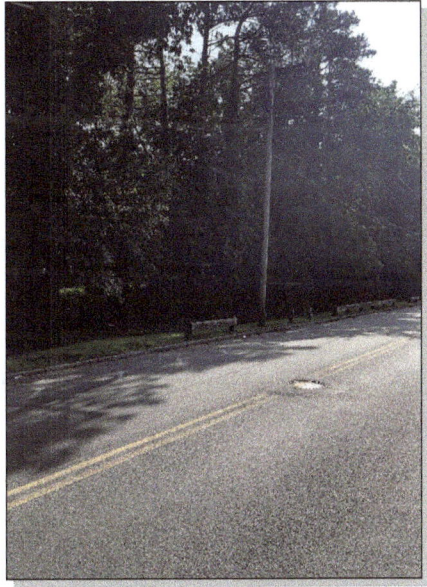

When The Call Arrived

It was the early 1990s, and I was about to leave for work. My partner Dick Urbanowicz gave me a call on my house phone and said, "Jim, we have an incident…. We need some photographs of a scene taken. Possible homicide down on Harmony Grove Road." Harmony Grove is a street that runs parallel to Boston Street in Salem. The location was right near the Salem-Peabody line.

The Backstory

Here is what we discovered and how this unfortunate situation unfolded. The victim in the case met up with this "gentleman," Calvin Daniels, and I use that term "gentleman" loosely. Calvin Daniel's father owned a gas station on Canal Street. It was a Texaco gas station. The story goes that one of the guys who worked for the father, Calvin Daniels Sr., was named Rick Boggs. Rick was working one day at the gas station and got hurt on the job. He then tried to begin the process of filing for workman's compensation due to injuries sustained on the job a few weeks earlier. The Daniels family did not like this one bit. In fact, Daniels Sr. disliked this so much that he went to his son and said, "Hey, can you take care of this situation for me?" So, what does that mean? "Take care of this situation?" Probably try and "talk him out of it" somehow? The father did not want to pay for this worker's compensation claim and was not sure if the business was carrying the requisite insurance or not. Remember, this was back in the early 1990s when Massachusetts's worker's comp laws were not as developed as they are today.

One Sunday morning, Calvin Daniels took a ride to Rick Boggs's house off Bridge Street in Salem. Somehow, he talked Rick into getting into his own car together. They then both drove off in Boggs's car and ended up on Harmony Grove Road at the Peabody/Salem line. As they were both sitting in the car, Calvin said to Rick Boggs, "Hey, you're going to have to drop this claim against my father's business." Boggs had issues with that demand and vocalized that to Calvin. It was at that point Calvin pulled out a gun.

From what we found out later, a struggle ensued after Calvin pulled out the gun, and it ended up going off. Rick Boggs got shot through the mouth and into his head. The bullet went right through his brain and lodged in the inner part of the skull. What we deduced was that Calvin must have panicked a bit at that time. As he got out of the vehicle, he thought of something better than just leaving him there. Calvin decided to go back inside towards Boggs and shoot him once more in the head.

At that point, Calvin got out of Boggs's vehicle and started walking down Harmony Grove Road towards Grove Street. He was seen by two people who were on their way to the laundromat. This turned out to be an important part of the case later.

Anyways, Rick Boggs's wife was at home at the time of the incident. Rick never came home, so she started to wonder where he was. Boggs's wife decided to take their other car and go look for Rick. She coincidentally drove down Harmony Grove Road and saw Rick's other vehicle parked on the roadside.

She pulled over, got out of the car, and started walking towards the car. She saw her husband lying, slumped over in the front seat. She immediately called the Peabody Police Department for a response. A young officer there responded to the scene and pulled Boggs out. Even though he was in a rigor mortis state, he attempted to do CPR on him to no avail. I always thought he did that just to appease Mrs. Boggs, who was also on the scene. It was at that time that I was called in by Detective Urbanowicz to take photographs, as it ended up being a Salem case.

The Scene

Telling this story today, I wanted to share with you, the reader, some of my thoughts about police work and what I remember about arriving at this scene. First, police work is hard and stressful. Police officers see the underbelly and dark parts of society that are shielded from everyday citizens. There are times among all the tragedies that police officers witness and deal with that some humor comes out. I mentioned this earlier in the book. Military and combat veterans can relate to this when "shit hits the fan". Sometimes you just need to chuckle. So, in this situation, the car door was open, and Boggs was lying on his back with his arm up in the air. When I arrived, he looked like a guy trying to change the back tire! It's funny what you remember after so many years.

Until the early-mid 1990s, the Salem Police Department outsourced film development for crime scenes, amongst other things. Can you believe that? Today, investigations are under such tight lock and key. Unless there was some sort of confidentiality arrangement in place, outsourced companies and their employees are not privy to this type of law enforcement information today. Anyway, this was how it was done back then, as we did not have great photo capabilities until the new police station was constructed. The film negatives were processed at a private photography business called Essex Camera located in downtown Salem. Pete Zaharis was the gentleman who owned and operated the place. He was our "go-to guy" for film development. He had the equipment and turned things around quickly for us.

Back to the investigation, Mrs. Boggs said the last person Rick was with was Calvin Daniels. Therefore, Calvin Daniels obviously became our prime suspect. We ended up teaming up with the Massachusetts State

Police and we eventually got Calvin to come into the old police station, located at 17 Central Street in Salem, to talk. You may wonder how we got Calvin to come in? It was nothing fancy; we just plainly asked him to come down! He did not push back or ask for an attorney. He was a little hesitant when he came in and sat down in one of our interview rooms.

At the table, we simply explained the situation that we were investigating, which was a possible homicide of someone that he had been seen with earlier that morning. The State Police led the interrogation with one of our senior Detectives, Dick Urbanowicz. As we were asking questions, I remember Calvin just sitting there listening, and we asked him directly if he would be willing to submit to a few chemical tests. He stared at us intensely, then asked what those tests were. We explained that we wanted to check and see if there were any blood splatter particles on his hands or some gunpowder residue. The gunpowder test is called a paraffin test. At that point, he decided to lawyer up and said, "I'm out of here." We did not have enough probable cause to hold him then or place him under arrest. So, we let him go, and he walked out freely.

Interesting Evidence

We found out later in the day through a guy that used to play on our Salem Police Softball Team (yes, police slow pitch softball was a thing back then, and yes, it is just like you would picture it... a bunch of 1980s cops wearing tube socks and short shorts) that Calvin Daniels was over in Beverly a few days earlier. He had a gun in his hand at the house of one of his "associates." Apparently, he saw a sheet metal type plate up on the wall. That plate was covering a hole that used to have a pipe connecting to it. Old heating system piping led to a hole in the wall for exhaust. Interestingly, people decorate these plates with scenes on them and stick them over the holes when not in use, or when decommissioned.

We received information from our source that Calvin shot a bullet into that decorative metal plate. The bullet went through and into the chimney stack where it dropped to the catch basin below down in the basement. When we learned that Calvin had done that, we immediately obtained a search warrant to go to that house and look for that bullet. When we arrived and searched the basin, there indeed was a bullet there in exceptionally good condition!

During the autopsy of Mr. Boggs, the bullets were retrieved from his head. The one that went through his mouth and lodged in the back of his skull was in good enough shape for ballistics to try and make a match with. The second bullet that went into his skull shattered into fragments.

A ballistics analysis was done between the bullet we found in the catch basin we retrieved and the clean bullet from Boggs's head. They matched up beautifully. At that point, we had enough probable cause to apply for an arrest warrant.

Arrest and Trial

We discovered in advance where Calvin would be on the day of the planned apprehension. He was located at the rear of Friendly's Ice Cream on upper Lafayette Street. A team of both State Police and Salem Police mobilized, apprehended, and brought him in with no incident. Once to the station, we planned to chemically test him for any remaining residue. However, we noticed that his arms were shaved from the mid-bicep all the way down to his wrist. They were completely cleaned, except for a bunch of scratches that were bleeding. It looked like he had taken a wire brush or something similar and scraped the hell out of his arms with bleach and probably other cleaning chemicals. He was well cut up, and finding blood was not a problem because it was his own and there was a lot of blood and scabs there. The tests came back negative as he cleaned himself up surprisingly well.

The trial ended up at Newburyport Superior Court, as courts frequently change venues. Sometimes it is Salem, other times Lawrence, etc. Newburyport just happened to be the venue for this trial. One thing I remember when walking into the court and waiting outside the courtroom itself were a few bigger guys who also walked in and stood in the hallway next to me. I recognized them immediately. They were opponents of mine in flag football, which I played every summer for many years. In fact, Calvin Daniels played on the same team as those guys as well... the Raiders. These two men were Calvin's brother, Teddy, and another guy. I asked them, "Hey, what are you guys doing here?" They replied, "Well, that's my brother on trial." I said to myself, "Oh, you got to be kidding me." There is a follow-on story to this.

Now to the start of the trial. Attorney Jacob Jones was Calvin Daniels's defense attorney. He was a well-known attorney in the area at the time and was hired by Calvin Daniels Sr. to defend his son. One distinct memory from that trial was the reverse, mirror imaged crime scene photos. Remember, I previously told you that the photos were developed via outsourcing through a local photo shop. Well, we sent out our photographs to be developed; the people at the photography lab inadvertently processed the photos in reverse order / position. In other words, the film had two sides, and the pictures came out mirrored. To explain, there is a shiny side, and there is a matte side. When the shiny side of the enlarger machine projects the photo down onto an easel, it becomes a positive photo. But if you turn the film over, the matte side is facing up, and the light shines down through onto the easel, and it becomes a positive photo in reverse.

When it was time for me to testify on the stand, Jacob Jones presented these mirrored photographs as evidence and asked me to observe them. He then said, "Do you recognize these photographs, Detective Gauthier?" I replied, "Yes sir, I do." Jones immediately fired back in a loud voice, saying, "And can you tell me if this is a fair and accurate representation of the scene?" I replied, "Yes, it is only in reverse." The judge turns around and said, "What the heck are you talking about?" The judge was sitting two or three feet away from me, and I could tell he was very irritated. So, I explained to him the film development process regarding shiny and matte and that it was a positive photograph but only in reverse.

Anyway, I got chastised for that aspect to try and weaken the investigative process. Police officers on the stand are always subject to being criticized by the defense attorney(s) quite often. The trial went on, and all the evidence was presented, which included the bullet and tons of circumstantial evidence because we never found the gun. We believe Calvin threw it in the ocean somewhere. So, this was mostly a circumstantial case, but this circumstantial case combined with the evidence led to the jury finding a guilty verdict of first-degree murder. I remember that as soon as the jury spokesperson said, "guilty in first degree," Attorney Jones stood up and said to the judge, "I would like to entertain that motion that we discussed." I wondered what "that motion" was, and when it was discussed. It seemed very odd to me. The judge and Jones knew each other socially. Not that knowing each other socially was a personal conflict of interest, but what happened next was rarely done in a courtroom. The judge overturned the guilty verdict without delay. Calvin Daniels walked out of Superior Court with a big shit-eating grin on his face like a man who knew he had beaten the system. We were disgusted as Detectives and investigators. We could not believe that the judge overturned the Jury's guilty verdict! It was confusing too!

Perhaps Attorney Jones convinced the Judge to think that the investigation by Massachusetts State Police and Salem Police was shabby. Perhaps it was a procedural issue. I do not quite remember. However, I do vividly remember the State Police being terribly upset by this because the ballistics techs matched the bullet perfectly from Boggs's head. The District Attorney Prosecutor was also extremely upset. The District Attorney at the time ended up appealing to the Judge's overturning of the conviction. The case was eventually brought back as a second-degree murder charge about one full year later.

The Year of Waiting

A few paragraphs ago, I mentioned that I was part of a flag football league and ran into some opponents at the courthouse. I played for the PJ's Pub flag football team out of Beverly, Massachusetts. PJ's Pub is no longer there. It has since been replaced by Fibber McGee's. Anyway, we had a fall game against the Raiders team I mentioned earlier. Calvin Daniels' brother Teddy, and the other guy from the courthouse hallway scene, were all on the Raiders team. The game was on a Sunday (which was about two weeks after the Newburyport trial). When we arrived and as my son Mike and I walked towards the sidelines, who did I notice? It was Calvin Daniels on the sidelines of the Raiders!

I approached him and said, "Hey, Cal, how are you doing?"

He mumbled back, "Yeah, I'm doing okay."

I asked, "Are you going to put a uniform on and play?"

"I don't know. I don't know," Calvin replied.

He did not put on a uniform that day, but we played the Raiders in the playoffs later that fall. Lo and behold, who had a uniform then, but Calvin Daniels!

I will say this… as a police officer, you must have a life too. I partook in recreational activities like anyone else, but there was a risk that you could always run into people from work, criminal cases, and other police situations. It was a coincidence running into Calvin on the field. Nonetheless, I was really excited about playing against him because I was going to be able to knock him around on the line. I was not worried at all, just pure excitement. As a police detective or a police officer, you are subject to people threatening you in your personal life, but that is part of having the job.

The game started, and Calvin was playing. I made sure that I got into a position where I was going to be opposite him on the line to block him after the snap. It was like a cat and a dog going against each other, with fur and dust flying. I tried to hit him as hard as I could because it is not too often you get an opportunity as a police officer off-duty to run into a bad guy like this. I got great personal satisfaction from blocking him and throwing some forearm shots in there! We ended up winning that game. A few days later, Calvin left for Florida.

At about the one-year mark after the judge overturned the guilty verdict, Calvin was "encouraged" by people he knew to come back to the Commonwealth because the Criminal Counsel overturned the non-guilty verdict. Calvin was rearrested at that time, and he was going to plead guilty to second-degree murder, which carried at the time of 5 to 20 years. The sentence structure worked out like this. He had to have served at least two-thirds of the bottom number of that sentence. So, if it were a 10-to-20-year term, he would have had to serve at least 7 – 7 ½. Also, he would have benefited from the time that he was already in jail. However, the law changed, and now an individual had to serve at least the bottom number before they were eligible for parole.

Calvin did not realize the change in law for whatever reason. When the court read the circumstances of the crime, he admitted that he did shoot Rick Boggs via a guilty plea. The judge sentenced him to 15 years without eligibility for parole until that term was complete. I remember hearing him say, "Hey, wait a minute. Wait a minute! I did not agree to this!" It was too late though, and he spent the next 15 years in Cedar Junction in Walpole, Massachusetts.

How It Ended

After a while, Calvin got paroled. While he was out, I learned that he broke into a house in West Peabody where a mafia kind of guy lived. He got caught for that and was sent back to jail to finish his original sentence. When he had completed fifteen years, he was released and got into trouble with his girlfriend shortly thereafter. There was a situation over in Beverly where she got dragged by his vehicle as he was driving away, which led to a parole violation. Now he is back in the system, serving a life sentence. All those cases added up. Occasionally, you see an article in the newspaper where he is applying again for parole, and he has been turned down several times over the years.

I'M SEARCHING YOUR HOUSE!

Location: 65 Mason Street
Coordinates: 42.52322* N, 70.90606* W

Back in the day, I worked with Sergeant John Moran, Head Detective at Salem PD. He planned to perform a search for drugs at this home in Salem. This was my first time delivering a search warrant, and being with John was exciting. Mind you, search warrants need to follow Massachusetts General Law, have probable cause that a crime has been committed, go through an application process, and have court approval. In other words, it is a whole process and procedure. Back in the '70s, there were times when that regulation or procedure was not 100% followed, and officers sometimes went rogue and just performed searches. That was how this particular search went.

Moran and I went to 65 Mason Street. There was a Hell's Angels member living there named Jerry Milton. John and I knocked on the door, Jerry opened, and we went in. Jerry Milton asked for the search warrant, and Moran showed him a piece of paper that said, "I'm searching your house," written on it. It was like something you saw in a movie! I couldn't believe it, but I let Moran go about his business. We were searching for drugs, as we had received a tip that there was heroin there. Moran had his sources of information, if you catch my drift, so we hit the house and found drugs. Jerry Milton was arrested.

A couple of years later, I ran into Jerry Milton, and I greeted him by his formal first name, Gerald.

He said to me, "Don't call me Gerald."

I replied, "But that is your name. Of course, I am going to call you Gerald."

He replied, "Nah, nah, call me Jerry."

I said, "No, I'll settle for Gerald."

So that was a little back and forth we had with me busting his chops. When I started in the police department, I did not know much about getting search warrants and all that stuff. The academy, local onboarding, and hands-on training was not like today. As the years went on, I had to learn a lot from trial and error and the experience of others. Law enforcement has advanced much since the '70s with policies, procedures, and regulatory updates. It was at that time of advancement when Moran retired. The '70s had their own standard operating procedures.

If the case were a murder or something to that level, things would be handled differently. This search warrant at Mason Street was like a sporadic, instantaneous kind of situation. It seemed more like harassment to Jerry Milton. Though I went along with the veteran detective as a rookie and I felt honored to work with Moran, I was somewhat confused about what I had just experienced!

SPLITTING THE MIDDLE

Location: *Liberty Hill Avenue*
Coordinates: *42.53571* N, 70.90527* W*

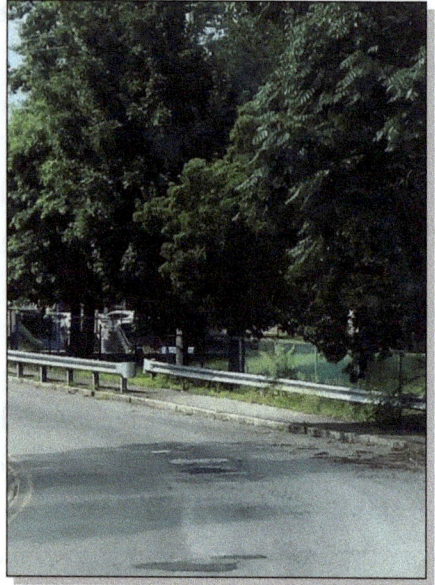

I'll never forget this story, as it was one of the luckiest outcomes in a vehicular accident I have seen in my police career in Salem. I was working in "3-Car" with my partner and got a call down to Liberty Hill Avenue for a motor vehicle accident. Right down a small hill past the Bates School, there's a pretty sharp curve in the road. What had just occurred was that two older ladies in their mid-seventies crashed right into the end of the guardrail. The ladies were driving from the Beverly Bridge along Kernwood Street at high speed and lost control of their vehicle when the street turned into Liberty Hill Avenue. The crash location is right on the sharp turn near the basketball court pictured above.

Here is the most amazing part. As I approached the car, I noticed that the guardrail went right through their engine block, impaled through the dashboard, and ended up right smack between the two old ladies. The rail split the middle of the car! I don't know how they did, but they both survived this high-speed crash without a scratch on them. Someone from above must have been looking out for them that day.

You may be asking yourself, "How did we extract both of the ladies from the mangled vehicle if metal was impaled right through it"? It was simple. They just got out of the car as usual. There was no need for the jaws of life or anything. They were in shock very badly, but eventually, they opened the door and got out on their own two legs. I asked them if they were okay. They told me they were but did not know what had just happened. I thought to myself, it was obvious what had just happened!

As my shift ended later that day, I kept thinking about that scene and this big chunk of guardrail metal impaling right through the car. It was a complete miracle they survived and were able to walk away from that scene unscathed like they did.

THE IMMOVABLE OBJECT

Location: 133 ½ North Street
Coordinates: 42.52812* N,
70.90319* W

Back in the 1980s, Robert St. Pierre, Conrad Prosniewski, some other detectives, and I all prided ourselves on tracking down bad guys, solving crimes, doing drug busts, and conducting search warrants. We were on a roll during this specific week and planned to conduct five drug search warrants in one night! Maybe this was an optimistic goal, but we decided to give it a go during the 4 PM – 12 AM shift.

One of the drug busts was up on North Street, where some Hell's Angels guys were living in a house that was slightly set back off North Street. Captain St. Pierre, who oversaw Detectives at the time, and I snuck across the front driveway area (as seen in picture) and up to the front door. We kept quiet, moved tactfully in the dark, and noticed that there weren't any house porch/spotlights on. There really weren't any motion sensor lights back in the day either. The front door was unlocked, and we silently crept up the front stairs to the second-floor landing. At the top of the landing, we saw the door we needed to breach.

At that point, Captain St. Pierre said to me, "All right, Jim, you're the door knocker. Time to take it down." What does the "door knocker" mean? It surely was not walking up to a bad guy's door and literally knocking. It was to breach the door aggressively. I want to quickly offer some perspective on being a police officer in the '80s. Back then, we did not have tactical breach gear like individual battering rams or explosive breaching-type stuff. As a matter of fact, there weren't really SWAT teams like they have today who are regionally organized, trained, and resourced. Sometimes, police departments have special operations units that train in this type of maneuvering. However, back then we local detectives conducted the raids and tactical type work ourselves!

When we breached doors, we just rammed them with our shoulders. Sometimes, we tried throwing a front-thrusting type kick if needed. My specialty, though, was the shoulder ram because it was like delivering a hit on the football field! I was the bigger guy on this raid at the time and had that role many times in the past. This was just another night! Back to the story, Captain St. Pierre whispered to me again, "Jim, take it down." I got my .38 caliber pistol out, held it in my hand, and ran as hard as I could into this door. BOOM! I hit that door, and I bounced off it like a trampoline. I ran back to the starting point to try again. Again, BOOM! I slammed the door hard and bounced off it once again!

I said to St. Pierre, "This is one hell of a door, Capt. It's not moving." The third time had to be the charm, so I backed up again one last time and rammed it. I bounced off a third time, and then St. Pierre said, "Oh Jim, wait a minute. I forgot they have that door barricaded by two, 2 X 4s on the other side." I chuckled and thought, oh my god, we had just telegraphed everything. In the meantime, we heard toilets flushing behind the doors. They knew we were outside in the hall. We decided to go to the other door on the second floor, and this time we knocked. We yelled, "Police! Open the door!" We couldn't ram this door in either, because it opened outwards. These bad guys had the entranceways planned well.

To sum this story up, we did end up getting into the apartment. The bad guys let us in and had a little smirk on their faces while they did. We knew that we had screwed up this time with the breach. All those times I bounced off the door gave them time to get rid of a good portion of their drugs. However, we did find some remnants, like some residue stuff lying around and some apparatus for measuring and cutting cocaine. These bad guys used a whiteish powder to cut down the potency of the cocaine. We did find some of that filler powder too. That night, we did make one arrest, but it was a very disappointing way to end the evening.

It made me think of how we prepared for raids back then. In that situation, we usually had some sort of informant that would purchase drugs for us and get the lay of the land inside the residence. The informants sometimes were actual drug users themselves who worked for us to make a few extra bucks. We used to give them marked cash to buy the drugs. When we got search warrants and did raids, we would look for the marked cash. That technique ties the drug dealers to the informant making the purchase. It was a common technique back in the day but certainly helped in evidentiary situations later in court.

A final interesting part about this story is that this was Captain Robert St. Pierre's last night of drug raids in his police career. As a matter of fact, the very week after that long night, Captain St. Pierre was sworn in as Salem's new Police Chief!

THE
DOWNTOWN
AREA

THE MAN ON THE STAIRS

Location: *266 Washington Street (Washington Sq)*
Coordinates: *42.51703* N, 70.89351* W*

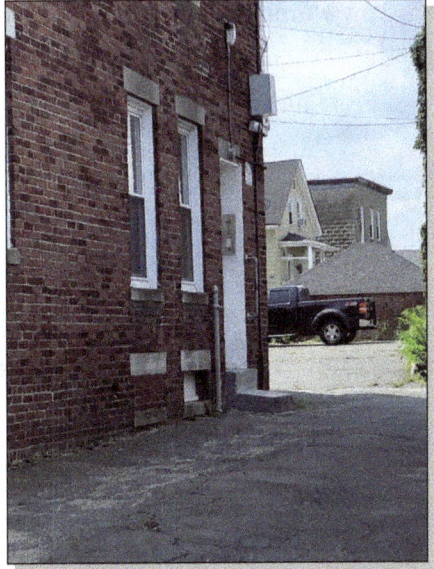

In the middle 1970s, my partner Dick Urbanowicz and I responded to a panicked call near Washington Square above the old Frame Shack store. The caller stated that there was an agitated man sitting on the stairway, holding a rifle. From what we understood, the man's ex-girlfriend had made the call and said to Dispatch that he would not let her out of the apartment and was not going to let anybody in. That was all the information we got at the time. Dick and I arrived at a three-family home and found out that the guy with the rifle was up in the 3rd-floor stairwell just as the caller stated.

As we entered the house on the ground floor, Dick said to me, "Jim, you know how to handle these situations. You go first." He knew that I was a United States Marine who had combat experience in Vietnam. I had no problem taking point. Although this was not the jungles of Vietnam at night on patrol, these situations are just as critical and unpredictable. I took out my .38 caliber revolver, went up slowly onto one set of stairs, and turned left on a small walkway. The stairs were configured in such a way that we needed to make a U-turn to go up the next flight.

The railing of the stairs had slats in it, so the person above could see us as we approached. There was the gunman sitting on the top of the stairs. We could see his foot through the slats. Also, we noticed that he was holding a British infield type of rifle. We needed to approach with caution. I had my weapon fully drawn and my finger on the trigger, then ran quickly to the bottom step, turned, and pointed my pistol directly at him!

I told him to "drop the rifle!" Fortunately, the rifle was lying across his lap and was not able to be fired at us. Again, I told him to "drop the rifle!" He hesitated, and I said one final time, "Drop the rifle, or I'm going to shoot!" Thankfully, he ended up slowly moving the rifle to his side, setting it on the stairs next to him. Dick and I then rushed in, secured the weapon, and cuffed him. We escorted him to the cruiser and made sure to check in with his ex-girlfriend upstairs as well before we left to ensure she was okay.

Today, this probably would be considered a formal hostage situation with major news coverage, helicopters flying everywhere, and regional SWAT teams being called in to handle this situation. Back in the '70s though, it was "just another day in the office" handled by officers like us.

THE OLD HOMES AREA

FEDERAL AND FLINT STREET CASE

Location: *146 Federal Street*
Coordinates: *42.52050° N, 70.90450° W*

Sometime in the 1980s, I was on-call for a week in the summer. I received a phone call from the police department that a woman had been sexually assaulted and that I needed to go to the Salem Hospital to meet and interview her. So I did, and discovered that this person was a woman in her middle seventies who was sexually assaulted by an individual at her house on Federal Street. At first, I thought to myself, what type of person would assault an older person like that? Next, I considered the possibility that this event may not have actually occurred. Perhaps, due to a senior impairment like dementia, this attack could have been all in her mind. I needed to learn more before making any assessment.

Upon arrival, I proceeded to the hospital room where she was resting. I introduced myself, spoke with her briefly, and documented her accounts. She explained that someone had broken into the house while she was sleeping in one of the side rooms. It was a male assailant who came in and sexually assaulted her. She fought him off and ended up being covered with bruises thereafter. When she was done being physically examined by the medical staff, I gave her a ride back home to Federal Street. Her house was the big yellow house on the corner of Federal Street and Flint Street.

As we drove down Munroe Street (where the Salem Library is located) and looked left onto Federal, we noticed that the Salem Fire Department was at her home! The back of the house was engulfed in flames! I'm thinking to myself, this poor woman was just assaulted, and she came back to her home being burned. It was a double whammy for her. She and I ended up getting in touch with her daughter, and she took her mother in for the evening. The mother ended up staying with her daughter for many months while her home was being repaired.

After the Fire Department finished their work at the burnt home, it was time for us to get investigating. Detective Jim Page and I went through the house looking for items we could possibly fingerprint. We looked for things that someone would touch, move around, or anything that might have been missing that we could follow up on at some point in the future. Unfortunately, we did not find much at all.

Through the ongoing investigation, we discovered that this man named Nelson Mandoval had broken into the house, stolen some items (VCR and DVD player), and conducted this sexual assault. Nelson had some documented emotional and mental issues. Apparently, when he left the victim's home, he walked down Flint Street towards Bridge Street and ran into another person he knew from the streets. Nelson told this person what he had done. This other person said to him, "Well, you need to get rid of the evidence, man. You probably left some evidence there." So, these two 'fine citizens' walked back up to the house, busted in through the back door, and entered a pantry area. In the pantry, some flammable, lighter fluid stuff was lying around. Nelson and his accomplice sprayed the liquid around the floor, and then they threw a match on it, hoping to rid any evidence of stolen items and the assault in general. The liquid set the rear of the house on fire hence the Salem Fire Department response.

Now, this accomplice to Nelson Mandoval was staying in an apartment down the other end of Flint Street. From that vantage point, one could see the victim's house down the other end of the street (on the corner of Federal and Flint). Nelson and his accomplice fled from the scene of the crime and hunkered at this other guy's apartment. These guys watched the house burn from a distance, thinking they had escaped the crime.

Months later, through our sources of information, we found out who that accomplice was and learned that he had moved out to Wisconsin.

Somebody that he knew told us, during our interviews and investigations, confirmed his exact whereabouts, and even provided an address for us. What service! Detective Page and I contacted the authorities out there, flew out, met them, and tracked that accomplice down to interview him. The man would not tell us anything about his involvement in this case back in Salem from months prior.

During those months of our investigation, Nelson Mandoval broke into an old age facility across the street from the old Salem jail, which today are apartments for the elderly (Fairview Apartments). When he broke into that place, he entered through a window and moved a plant. The plant was artificial, so he left very nice fingerprints on it when he touched it. I was able to successfully lift clean fingerprints off it and Nelson Mandoval was charged with breaking and entering that apartment. The case went to court, and he was incarcerated at the Essex County Jail.

While incarcerated, Nelson felt guilty about a crime he said that he had committed in the past. He wanted to talk to the Salem Police Detectives about it. Detective Page and I went to the Essex County Jail to speak with him. Surprisingly, he admitted that he was the one who broke into the house and sexually assaulted the older woman on Federal Street months prior. He felt so guilty inside that he was compelled to talk. He said, "God would not forgive me unless I told you about what I had done." We asked him additional open-ended questions to further inquire. Again, he confessed again that he was the one who burned the home and sexually assaulted the woman.

Detective Page and I felt a lot of emotion as we had investigated this case for quite a while. We got to know the victim and her daughter quite well after several months of staying in touch, meeting up, and giving her updates on our progress. It was a full year of doing this until the case went to trial. Nelson pleaded guilty in court, and he received something like 25 years, or what we used to call "Telephone Book Numbered Sentence," in jail. Finally, some justice had been served.

Following the sentencing and incarceration, we all knew the victim could rest a little more easily, knowing that this individual was off the street. The victim was now safe, and she could go on with her life. She ended up moving back into the house after it was repaired and lived out her life for another ten years or so. She passed away, but we always kept in touch with the daughter. The daughter always remained grateful for the efforts Page and I put in. We appreciated that.

Regarding the accomplice who moved to Wisconsin, since we couldn't find any substantial evidence at the scene, we had only Nelson's word and that would not have stood up in court. Therefore, charges were never brought against the accomplice.

FLINT STREET DOOR BUSTING

Location: 33 Flint Street
Coordinates: 42.51947* N, 70.90427* W

We did a drug raid on Flint Street one night. This house was (and still is) set back from the main street, and from the informant we used for intelligence, we knew that there were two doors that had to be broken down first to get into the apartment. The apartment was located on the second floor as well. A few detectives and I walked down the narrow driveway and up to the first door. We mobilized outside the entrance door to the apartment building itself. I ran up and knocked that one down off the hinges. Next, we sprinted up to the front door of the apartment itself. With my gun drawn, I hit that door and went right through the center panel and ended up in a folded over position. There were a few individuals just nonchalantly sitting at the kitchen table. Then their expression turned from lackadaisical to shock!

I popped up and stated I was a police officer and for them to stay put with their hands visible. The other detectives and I immediately proceeded to search the people to ensure there were no weapons on them. We provided the search warrant and then proceeded to search the apartment fully. We ended up finding the drugs we heard of. They were hidden inside of a dirty diaper that was in a pale. We had information ahead of time that drugs would possibly be located there. It was a good quantity of cocaine.

This successful raid would not have been possible without the intelligence from a solid informant or two. These confidential and reliable informants we had back in the day made our job as detectives more successful than it would have been completely on our own. In some cases, informants would proactively contact us with leads and tips about drugs and other illegal activity. In other instances, informants really enjoyed working for us and making a few bucks for themselves. With that raid the informant we used was supplied with money and bought drugs at that apartment weeks earlier. We paid them a fee for their services. These informants were typically shady characters. Sometimes, they would try and pinch a little bit of drugs off the top. We would call them out on that if we ever caught them. We straightened them out quickly by reminding them they could be charged for a crime they had just committed.

"GET DOWN, GET DOWN!"

Location: *36 Warren Street*
Coordinates: *42.51765* N, 70.90437* W*

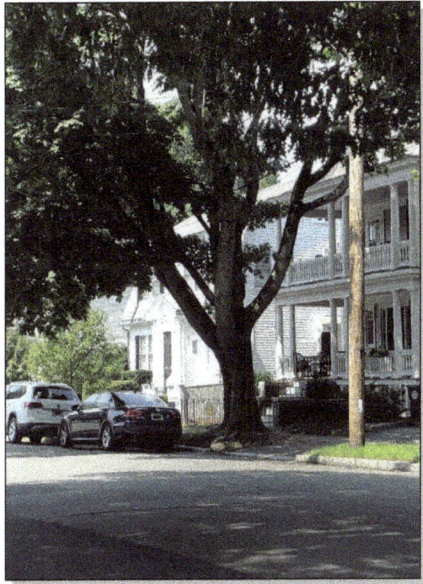

One Sunday morning, my partner Dick Urbanowicz, gave me a call. I was home then, and he said, "Jim, you got to come in quickly!" I had a pair of gym shorts, and a short sleeve, floral, green, and yellow Hawaiian shirt on. I did not really have time to change and needed to make it quickly to the station. Once I arrived, Urbanowicz and I rushed down to the surveillance van parked in the back lot. The Salem Police at the time had an unmarked van with tinted windows that were mirrored outwards.

We drove across town over to Warren Street. What I found out was that there was going to be a drug delivery of heroin. The information we received was that over a hundred bags of heroin were going to change hands and be delivered to a house on one of the side streets. We pulled up in our van across the street from where we thought the drug dealer might be coming from. We just sat and waited.

Sure enough, an individual pulled up across the street and he was identified as the person of interest. He got out of his car, and Urbanowicz and I jumped out of the van! We pulled our weapons out, hustled towards him with our guns drawn, and screaming for him to "get down, get down!" He had a paper bag in his hand at the time, and he fell onto the ground on the sidewalk. As we got closer to him, we knew that he was terrified and visibly upset because we could smell the odor of feces on him. He had shit his pants when we were coming towards him with guns drawn. We ended up arresting the guy and charging him with major trafficking of heroin. He had around 140 bags of heroin on him.

The police department immediately obtained a search warrant for that house on the side street, and we conducted a raid later that morning. Inside the home, we found more heroin. A young couple was living there, waiting inside to receive the drugs, and they were also terrified when we raided the home. We arrested them as well and brought them in.

STANDING STILL

Location: *329 Essex Street*
Coordinates: *42.52073*N, 70.899981*W*

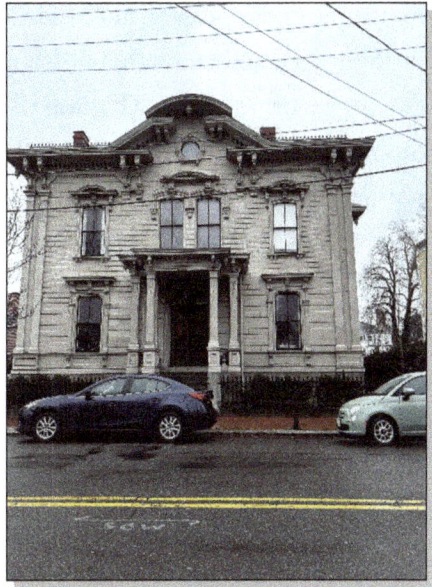

This short story is a little strange. It took place during a time when I was working patrol sometime between 1974 and '81. On Essex Street, a little ways past the main library, but on the opposite side of the street, there was a little rooming / multi-tenant house (see picture). Dick Urbanowicz and I were getting through with our overnight shift in the early morning. It was still dark outside, and the sun was slowly rising. It was wintertime too. As Dick and I were driving by that rooming house back to the station, we looked up, and there was a light on illuminating the second floor. We saw this man standing there, very still. He was not moving at all, just standing there. We just thought he was looking at something like the television or whatever. We drove by and went into the station to be relieved by the day shift.

We both went home to get some sleep as we needed to come back to work at 4 PM later. When Dick and I started the shift again, it was once again dark in the afternoon. We started our patrol route, and as we drove down Essex Street around 5 PM, we looked up and saw that the light in that room was still on. The guy was still standing in the same position. We thought that that was kind of unusual at this point. We both agreed that we needed to check this out.

Dick and I pulled over and parked our cruiser. We then went through the common door, walked up the stairs, and found the man's room. We knocked on his door. No answer. Again, we knocked, no answer. We then forced the door open and got inside. Unfortunately, there was a gentleman in there deceased and hanging from the light fixture with his feet about two inches off the floor. That was the reason he did not move all day long. Strange. We called the morgue and had him taken away. His family was notified, and we hoped the man could then rest in peace.

THERE IS SOMETHING PARANORMAL GOING ON

Location: *The Pickering House, 18 Broad Street*

Coordinates: *42.51842* N, 70.90027* W*

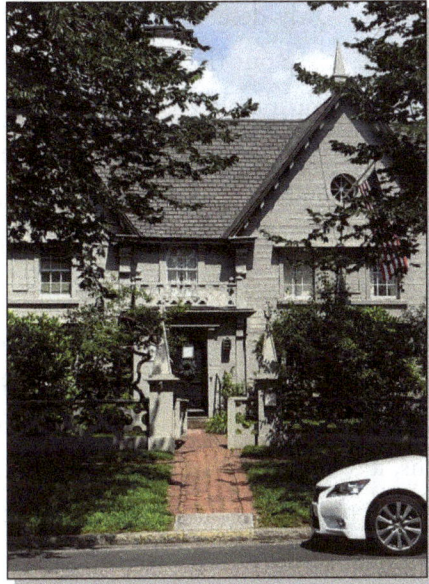

Back in the 1970s, we were on patrol and received a call that there was a possible breaking and entering at a historic home in downtown Salem. The home is called The Pickering House. This house is one of the oldest homes in Massachusetts, dating back to the early 1660s. It was built by John Pickering, who was a carpenter from England. To say the least, this was a unique call.

My partner, Dick Urbanowicz and I arrived at the scene and walked the property to see if there was anything out of place. We went around the side of the house and back to the rear. The back door was open, so we slowly entered the home to investigate further. This was the first time that either of us had set foot in this historic home. Back then, it was occupied by the Pickering family and was not open to the public like it is today.

Dick and I were in awe of this place mainly due to its historical significance. Still, we knew we needed to investigate and explore the upstairs, main floor, and the basement for unusual activity and disturbances. Upstairs looked fine, with no disturbances or signs of theft. The main floor looked fine as well. Next was the basement.

The basement door was a very small, colonial-type door from hundreds of years ago. It was narrow as well. Dick and I opened the door, squeezed through it somewhat sideways, turned on our flashlights, and began slowly descending the stairs. We did not see any light switches or anything, so our flashlights were the only source of light. Down we went into the musty, old basement that had dirt floors.

Once we were at the bottom, we looked around a bit. The basement had old granite columns and foundation blocks around the edges. It was very historical. The ceiling was low, probably around five and a half feet. Certainly, it was shorter than we were tall because we were crouching a bit. While we were down there, Dick and I noticed something a little odd. It was an odd feeling that we experienced at the same time! We both felt an instant cold chill with a little air movement. Almost a light breeze. To us, it felt like there was an old spirit hanging around down there. It was a very creepy feeling, and we both felt something was down there with us like a ghost/spirit of some sort. We looked at each other with that look of concern and read each other's mind… it was time to head back upstairs and get the heck out of there! We were happy to report back that we did not find any signs of B&E.

We finished up the night and reported back that the wind opened the back door of the Pickering House. It was a rainy and stormy type of night, so it made sense that a door could have flung open. I have never returned to that house for a call, or any other reason. To be honest, I never had a desire to go back after that basement experience. Considering that many places in Salem have reported paranormal activity over the years, what we experienced could have been just that!

THE POINT
AREA

OPERATION SNOW REMOVAL

Location: *Various*
Coordinates: *Various*

L et me tell you about Operation Snow Removal, one of our most known drug removal operations due to the branding/ marketing of the operation, as well as the press coverage it received. This operation all started because, down the Point Area of Salem, there was a large amount of cocaine being distributed. We were getting reports that cocaine was actually being distributed brazenly in the streets! Some streets of significance were Dow Street, Prince Street, Palmer Street, Park Street, and Harbor Street. Salem Police had to do something about this. We Detectives strategized with our superiors and decided that a joint Massachusetts State Police and Salem Police operation was the best move forward. We got in touch with the State Police, and this is how the operation went down.

The State Police had some undercover agents that were going to go down to the Point and try and make some buys from the drug dealers. However, we needed to record it. We needed to visualize what was going on. Fortunately, one of the neighbors in the area allowed us to use their enclosed porch outside on the second floor of their apartment building. It was a good spot, and we had a perfect view of Dow Street, where most of the activity was taking place. We set a video camera up and had it pointing down on the area. It was wintertime, and Billy Jennings and I did most of the observing from the cold, non-insulated porch.

While we were observing the area, we knew when the State Police undercover officers would pull up in their unmarked cars and make a buy. The undercovers did that several times, and each time, dealers would come up, sell their cocaine, and the car would drive off. We'd document all that on video and take written notes as well. The State Police did their documentation too. We did this repeatedly over a several-week period. One of the times that we were up there, we saw a 10-year-old boy delivering the drugs to the undercover vehicle. Billy and I said to ourselves, "Son of a gun, just a 10-year-old boy out there dealing the drugs for the drug dealer himself?" That really got us upset.

At the end of the surveillance and purchases of drugs, we counted several individuals involved. I think there were probably eight or ten people that we observed dealing drugs in that area. After a period of a month or two, arrest warrants were issued for all those individuals. It was at this time we went on to the big operation, "Operation Snow Removal." We just swooped in and scooped the bad guys like a snowplow clearing the snow (cocaine) off the roads in the dead of winter. The name of the operation was a great play on words.

I made sure to have a "little talk" with the bad guy who had the 10-year-old boy dealing his drugs. I made the strong point to him that we did not appreciate him using little kids to make a profit for himself. Absolutely despicable.

About six months to a year later, the cocaine and heroin business was picking up again in the neighborhood. Again, we ended up setting surveillance down there and used the same strategy, having the State Police come in and do the undercover purchases. This time, there was going to be a bust happening onsite. There was one person, a woman who was known to the Salem Police as a notorious drug dealer. Her name was Linda, and she was a heavyset woman. As we watched the drug bust, one of the State Police Detectives (another larger person like a football player) was partaking in the upcoming raid in this tiny, unmarked vehicle. I mean, this vehicle was tiny. I'm unsure of the make or model, but it was comparable to one of those Minis you see today. The plan was that the Detective was going to invite the woman dealer into the tiny car to sell to him.

Observing from the porch with Billy Jennings, we watched the woman dealer get into the vehicle along with this State Police Detective from

Danvers. The whole side of the car went down six inches, and you could hear us laughing on the surveillance video. The situation was one you had to be there for. It was such a serious situation, but the combination of a teeny clown car being used, and two large individuals you would never see getting into a car like this in real life, was too much for us to handle. I mean, the car's height was lowered by half a foot, and we did not expect that! Billy and I chuckled for a while and totally forgot about the camera mic being live! Operation Snow Removal 1 and 2 were basically the same strategy repeated the same way. Both operations captured eight to ten individuals each, so close to 20 dealers in the Point area were arrested.

With respect to the raids, warrants were issued for the 20 dealers and most of them went smoothly and mostly peacefully. There was one, though, on Congress Street that was not so peaceful. We went to find an individual and to search his apartment. It was a tag team with the State Police and several of our Salem Detectives. We knew the Point neighborhood had bad guys on the lookout for police activity, so a huge caravan of unmarked cars would draw attention. Due to the fact we needed a larger vehicle for the whole team, we decided to rent two huge U-Haul trucks. It was less conspicuous, and they held a lot of people. There were probably 20-25 of us back there in total with two K9s as well.

We drove the trucks down onto Congress Street and pulled into one of the parking lots next to the subject's apartment building. We opened the van door and jumped out like a mad herd of cops. We hit two or three different apartments that we planned to raid, and it went down so fast. We just operated. We found a multitude of drugs on the raids, and on one of them, we found over one hundred grams of cocaine inside of a sock in a top dresser drawer. Also, a large amount of cash was there too.

Inevitably, we found weapons as well during the raids. This one raid we did took us to the basement area of one of the large apartment buildings down the Point. The basement is connected to the whole building and was probably 25 to 30 yards long, with several different storage bins all around. Believe it or not, we found a pile of feces on the floor, and under the feces was a large package of cocaine. The bad guys figured that nobody would ever think to look under a pile of crap, but we had information that there was cocaine in that spot if you could believe it! Drugs were found in a lot of crazy places.

In the end, a bunch of 20 low-level dealers made plea deals for leniency, so we could work to get the bigger fish off the street later. A couple of them were prosecuted based on the trial outcomes. We celebrated the successful operations by posing with a big chalkboard in our room, drawing a picture of a plow pushing drug dealers off the street. In fact, the picture shows the dealers flying in the air off the street. There are a few photographs of us Detectives all together celebrating. Again, we tried to add a little bit of humor to our day-to-day when appropriate. There was enjoyment in the profession back then being a cop. We were proud of the work we did to keep the City of Salem safer.

PARK AND HARBOR STREET FIRES

Location: 16 Park Street, and 59 Harbor Street
Coordinates: Various

My partner, Urbanowicz, and I were in the #22 car, which was a station wagon. We were patrolling on Harbor Street, heading toward Lafayette Street. As we drove by Park Street, we looked over and noticed flames coming out of a second-story window of Unit #16. I called the fire department right away. However, since we were the first ones on the scene, we had to do something. We pulled the cruiser in front of the residence that was on fire and thought quickly about how to get into this building and to the second floor.

I decided I was going to enter the building, so I ran as fast as I could from across the street, up several stairs, barged through the door, and went inside the building. It was a little smoky, for sure. Next, was to make it up to the second floor. On my hands and knees, I worked my way up to the next level. Flames were shooting up on the ceiling, and embers were dropping down on me. The smoke was extremely intense at this time, so I tried to stay as low as possible. Finally, when I arrived at the second door unit I banged on the door. The woman who lived there, came out frantic and naked from a back bedroom. I told her to quickly head to the back stairs of the building to escape. The Fire Department met her with blankets and oxygen.

Before she left the building, she told me that her son was in the back room. Quickly, I made my way through the smoke to the back room, and as I went inside, the Fire Department was already coming through the window via the ladder truck from the outside! We both grabbed the boy, and a few firemen took him out the window and down the ladder. I crawled back out on the floor, down the stairs, and proceeded to go outside. Breathing was difficult, so I was rushed to the ER for smoke inhalation. They immediately applied oxygen to me upon arriving, and my breathing turned around for the better. The boy and the mother were both safe, and the Fire Department successfully extinguished the fire.

Another fire that occurred was over at 57-59 Harbor Street. My partner, George Canney, and I encountered a large apartment that was constructed as a complex brick building. We arrived at the scene around one or two o'clock in the morning. It was a really difficult situation because families on the second and third floors needed to get out ASAP. George and I went around the back, grabbed a ladder from the fire department, who had just arrived, and set it up on the

second-floor porch in the rear of the building. The residents climbed over the porch and came down the ladder safely.

The Fire Department guys were having difficulty getting the hoses up to the second and third floors to start working the fire. First, George and I hoisted the ladder to the third-floor porch, but it was a little short for the family to escape. Canney climbed up onto the porch and I went up the back stairs. Both Canney and I led the family out of the burning building at this time. Then we helped with the hoses (that were heavy and full of water at the time) and snaked our way through the back stairs up to the second and third floors. George and I then walked from the rear of the apartment to the front. We found ourselves in a hallway, and the flames were coming up the stairs. We were going to be trapped. George and I looked at each other and made a command decision to get the hell out of there! At any moment, the whole front stairway and porch section was going to collapse. Thankfully, we dodged flames and made it out of there safely.

Unfortunately, when we got back out onto the street, the Fire Department personnel took out two children who had tragically succumbed to the smoke and the flames. It was a tragic day altogether, but it certainly could have been much worse. It was one of the worst fires aside from the Flynn Tannery that I've seen in my career.

MAY 30, 1978

FROM: THE OFFICE OF THE CHIEF
TO: OFFICERS URBANOWICZ, GAUTHIER, VERRETTE
SUBJECT: COMMENDATION

Your performance on May 26, 1978 at 16 Park St. whereby you
no doubt were responsible for saving several lives during a serious
fire at the afore-mentioned address is commended by this office.
Your disregard for your own safety during this incident is appreciated by your community.

Well done,

Charles J. Connelly
Chief

CJC:sl
cc:Bulletin Board
   Capts. Boyajian, Coughlin
   Personnel files

READ AT ROLL CALL

SALEM POLICE DEPARTMENT
SALEM, MASSACHUSETTS

MARCH 13, 1981

TO: CHIEF CHARLES J. CONNELLY
FROM: EXECUTIVE OFFICER, CAPT. MURRAY GREENLAW
SUBJECT: COMMENDATIONS

I wish to recommend Officer James Gauthier for an individual commendation for his actions, that are to be considered above and beyond the call of duty at a General Alarm Fire at 51-55 Harbor St. on March 7, 1981 at 3:30 A.M.

Off. Gauthier did assist the firemen in bringing a ladder to the rear of the burning buildingand while the firemen were busy trying to break through a bolted rear door, with Off. Canney raised the ladder to the second floor window and assisted a Mr. Rodriquez to the ground. Then observing several people trapped on a balcony on the third floor, with Off. Canney, raised the ladder to this balcony, but it was a little too short. When Off. Canney climbed the ladder and entered the building, Off. Gauthier went to the rear door that had been opened and with some firemen entered the burning building. They fought their way up the stairs, where they met Off. Canney, a young girl, two boys and a man and led these people to safety. Then with Off. Canney, Off. Gauthier reentered the building and began breaking windows with their flashlights. When the ceiling started to fall on them, they started to leave the building, but were met by some firemen bringing a hose line to the third floor. These officers helped the firemen bring the hose to the third floor. At this time, Off. Gauthier with Off. Canney had to leave the building because they could not stand the smoke any longer. Off. Gauthier returned outside and assisted the victims of the fire.

The Salem Police Department is very proud of the professional actions of this officer.

Respectfully submitted,

Capt. Murray Greenlaw
Executive Officer

MG:sl

LAFAYETTE STREET AREA

DEAD MAN'S CURVE

Location: *Corner of Fairview Avenue and Lafayette Street*
Coordinates: *42.49824* N, 70.88855* W*

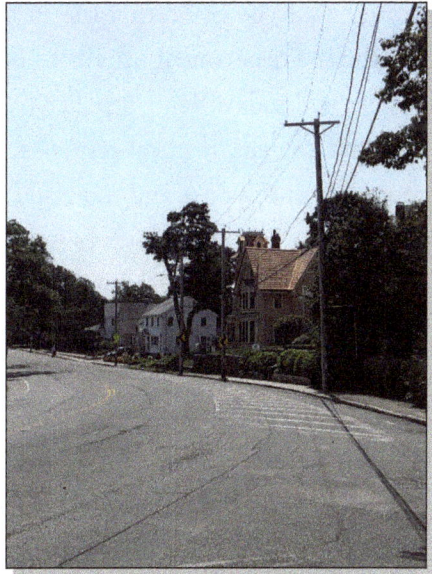

I was working on the upper 5 beat (that's a beat where you work by yourself in the cruiser) patrolling on Lafayette Street. The "beat" means a territory in Salem that different officers were assigned to. There is a curve called "Dead Man's Curve" at the bottom of Lafayette Street near the Lead Mills. That evening, there was a report of a motor vehicle accident at Dead Man's Curve. I was patrolling around the Forest River Park area at the time but responded immediately to the call.

When I arrived, I found a vehicle plowed into a telephone pole with a woman behind the wheel. This young woman was in her early twenties, maybe even late teens. I ran over, quickly analyzed the scene, and realized that the telephone pole had gone right through her engine block. It pinned her foot under the brake pedal! In other words, the pole pressed the front end of the car directly against her foot. Her shin bone was snapped at a 90-degree angle, and she was trapped in there pretty good.

There was no way to get her out without moving the vehicle away from the telephone pole to try and decompress her leg. Very quickly, I had to devise a method of getting the vehicle off the pole without further injuring her leg, noticing that she was a little bit under the influence and certainly in a state of shock. Other cruisers also just arrived to close off the road and stop traffic. This gave me an idea of how to set her free, which had to do with tow trucks. I made the call for two tow-trucks to come down to the scene.

It should be noted that the city did not have paramedics back then, but the fire department usually responded to these types of incidents like they would today. Being a police officer back then was like a 3-in-1 job: law enforcement, medical response, and security. Today, there is a much more robust response and more specialization. However, I was trained as an EMT so I could perform basic medical services.

When both tow trucks arrived, I was now ready to implement my idea. It was a tense situation where every minute mattered because the woman's leg shin was broken. The longer we waited, the more chance of infection and possibly a future amputation, or worse. I instructed each of the trucks to hook up to each corner of the rear of the woman's vehicle. On my command, I directed them to both pull an inch back at a time from opposite directions (one side to the other).

Inch by inch on my commands, the trucks pulled the car back symmetrically so that the pole was off her leg! The Fire Department then used the "jaws of life" to cut the roof off. We all helped extract and transport her to Salem Hospital. Over the next couple of days, my partner Gary Lynch and I went up to the hospital to check on that woman. The doctors saved and repaired her leg, which was great to see. The woman told us that she was very grateful for the Police and Fire Department's efforts in extracting her without further damaging her leg.

About 20 years later, I was at Eastern Bank using their ATM. As I was walking out of the front door, I noticed a van pulled up right in front.

A woman jumped out of the van towards me and asked, "Are you Officer Gauthier?"

"Yes, I am," I replied.

It was at that moment I recognized who it was. We chatted for a moment, and she thanked me again for the situation 20 years before. She said she never forgot me, and my coming to the hospital was special to her. We gave each other a big hug and went on our way. I forgot her first name but seeing her living a normal life after all those years was rewarding.

IT WAS NOT THAT FRIGID

Location: *Lafayette Street at the Old Lead Mills*

Coordinates: *42.49757* N, 70.888690* W*

It was wintertime in late February, and I was working by myself in a patrol car covering the "Upper 5" areas by Salem State College. I received a report of a van that had landed in the water down by the Lead Mills. Apparently, a woman was driving a van with someone she had met in Marblehead. From what I found out later, it was the gentleman's van she was driving. She was intoxicated driving back over to Salem and coming down the hill (It's quite a steep decline over there!) from Marblehead, probably about 60-70mph from what we figured out. She lost control, veered off the road right between a telephone pole and a tree, hit the guardrail, went flying airborne through the air, and landed about 35 feet into the inner harbor area (see picture of the site)!

At the time, it was high tide, and the vehicle was half-submerged in the water. The man who was in the vehicle with the woman got out, swam to the rocks ashore, and left her stranded behind the wheel. What a caring guy he was! When I arrived, and other cruisers started showing up, he told me a woman was inside the van. Without hesitation, I took off my gun belt, ran down the embankment, jumped down onto the rocks, and jumped into the water. The water was frigid, probably 40 degrees or so. I knew I had to act fast to save the woman but not get hypothermia and succumb to the elements myself.

Upon reaching the half-submerged van, I somehow managed to get the passenger side door open with a hard pull. It's tough to pull open a door when it's submerged. The woman was on the driver's side but leaning over towards the passenger side, which put her in an awkward position for me to help her. The van at this time was submerging even more so now. I'm not sure of the depth in that part of the harbor during high tide, but somewhere around 8 to 10 feet was likely. I did not want to hang out there any longer, so I ended up grabbing her with two arms around the torso and under the armpits and yanked her out.

Getting back to shore was a struggle. Luckily, the Fire Department just arrived. They lowered the basket down to me over the 8-foot embankment, and I secured the victim in place with straps. She suffered a broken leg in the accident, come to find out. The Fire Department pulled her up and took her off to the hospital where she survived. An ambulance took me to the hospital as well, where I did suffer from hypothermia but made a full recovery myself. It took spending a few hours in the ER wrapped in blankets to get my body temperature regulated. After I recovered later that night, I drove myself back home, changed into some new clothes, and spent the rest of my shift in bed. The Officer in Charge gave me the rest of the night off.

A few weeks after that incident, the woman called the police department and thanked me for my efforts that night in helping her out. I never knew what happened to the van and how they pulled it out of the harbor area. Also, I never found out about the guy who left the woman behind.

Hopefully, they did not ask each other about going on a second date. That relationship was cursed from the start!

SCARY SITUATION, SMART VICTIM

Location: *233 Lafayette Street*
Coordinates: *42.51164* N, 70.89227* W*

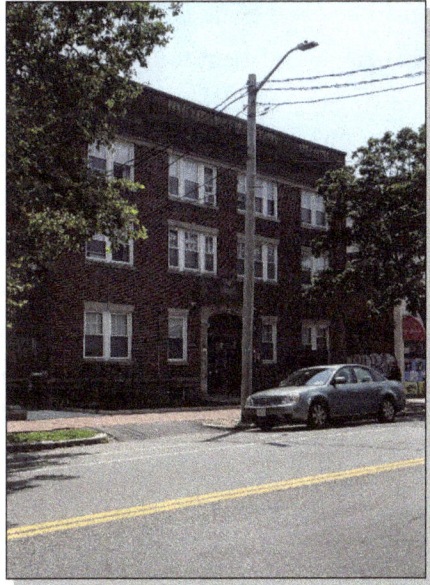

This is quite a story and certainly memorable for me because of the way this victim acted during an extremely scary situation. In the early '80s, my partner and I received an urgent call from the station that a young woman had been kidnapped and assaulted. She was at her apartment over at 233 Lafayette Street. We found that strange because if someone were kidnapped, they usually wouldn't be at their own house or apartment. Nevertheless, we had to see what was going on over there.

My partner and I pulled up to the small apartment building, got out of the cruiser, and walked through the front door into the common/lobby area. There was a guy standing in the downstairs hallway just kind of hanging out, which was also a little weird. This hallway was not a place to really hang out. There were no places to sit, and it did not have a "common area" feel to it. We checked him out, went up the stairs, and knocked on the woman's door. The woman answered the door; she was probably a young lady in her early twenties. She quietly relayed to us that she had been up in Newburyport earlier in the day and had met a guy. That guy ended up grabbing, hitting, and kidnapping her by pulling her into his car. He tied her up and laid her down sideways in the backseat.

Amazingly, she managed to somehow convince the predator that she wanted to stay with him and be with him. She stated she wanted to be his girlfriend and escape with him, but he would need to drive her back to her apartment in Salem so she could get some clothes first. She was smart and convincing, and the man agreed to drive her back to Salem. When they arrived, he stopped in front of her apartment building and then let her go into her apartment to get her clothes.

This guy waited in the hallway for her. Interestingly, the man never went up the stairs to check on her. He just let her go unchaperoned. When she did enter her apartment, she locked the door and called the police. That's how convincing she was, or how gullible he was. We then realized that the guy we saw in the hallway downstairs was the same guy she was telling us about. We did not think he would have been hanging around like he was, especially when two uniformed cops entered.

After we were sure she was okay, we immediately went back downstairs looking for him, but he was gone. My partner and I went outside, turned on our flashlights, and started looking around the sidewalk. We then turned to the right and walked down the sidewalk towards downtown Salem. We found the guy hiding in the bushes just another house or two away. I thought to myself, why would he still hang around the area and hide in the bushes? We ended up placing him into custody, and a few months later, this case went to trial. He was found guilty of kidnapping and sexual assault.

Coincidently, this was the first sexual assault charge for the prosecutor (Assistant District Attorney) and I in our careers. We both discussed together after the trial was over and we agreed that it was amazing how that female victim kept her wits about her during that ordeal.

WORLDWIDE NEWS

Location: *23 Gardner Street*
Coordinates: *42.51337* N, 70.89451* W*

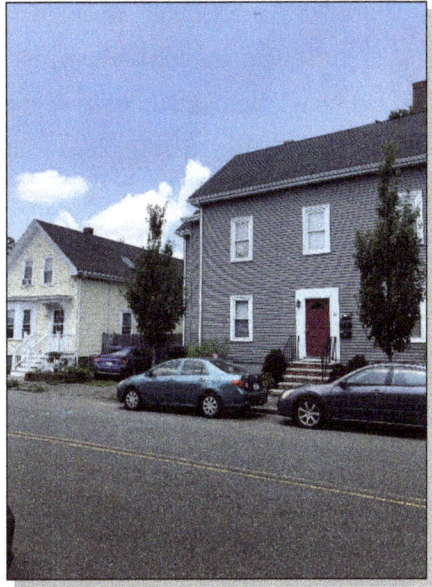

It was the middle 1970s, and a call came in midday about a disturbance at 23 Gardner Street, which is right off Lafayette Street. My partner and I were in 2-Car at the time, which patrols Salem's "Point" area and a little bit of Lafayette Street. As we arrived at 23 Gardner, I walked up the front steps, went into the hallway area, and knocked on the apartment door. No one answered. I knocked again and again, but there was no answer. At that point, we were concerned about the safety of the people and anyone who was inside, as our police response was due to a disturbance call. We then entered and turned left into the living room.

Right there in front of us was an impaled green and red parrot stuck to the wall with a crossbow arrow. Someone had fired a shot at an airborne parrot! I first thought of who and why someone would do something like this. Was there some other meaning to this? I thought this because, on the other wall on the other side of the room, there was a huge pentagram smeared with blood. There were also another few pentagrams painted on the floor. Something eerie was going on there before we arrived.

It was not up to us to find out what type of cult activity was happening here and to investigate down some strange rabbit hole. However, we did need to hold the person accountable for killing that parrot. We had enough probable cause to hold the individual accountable for the animal killing. We obtained a summons for him to appear in court on charges of cruelty to animals.

Probably a week later, this exact story got picked up in the local newspaper and then, a few days later, by the Associated Press and the Weekly World News tabloid. My partner told me about it in the office about this sensational article regarding heavy satanic ritual activity going on in Salem! We never really knew if this was true satanic activity that occurred inside 23 Gardner. Still, surely the tabloid highlighted it to the max, but we did find out that the man who was charged with animal cruelty was a member of a cult-type of community. So, it could have been a possibility.

In the 1970s and '80s, there were only so many ways to research things like today. Salem has always been a haven for subculture type of community, even back then. We did not know much about this cult-community and had limited research capabilities, but we knew it was present back then. There were other open, satanic-type houses of worship throughout the city and in my 32-year career at Salem Police Department, I never had a criminal case or problem with the Wiccan community either. There were occasions, when we found pig hearts and chicken bones burnt on a small rock cliff down at Forest River Park, but we found out through an investigation that it was some type of cultural activity.

Salem sure is a melting pot of highly peculiar cultures. However, these cultures are just communities that do their best to assimilate into the general population. Back in the day, Salem was accepting, but not so much as it is today.

"YOU GOTTA GO UP THERE, JIMMY BOY"

Location: *326 Lafayette Street*
Coordinates: *42.50599*N, 70.89119*W*

In the mid-late 1970s, I was at roll call over at the Police Department and received a call to go up to the top end of Lafayette Street near Salem State University ("College" at the time). When I arrived at the home at 326 Lafayette Street, an older gentleman who wanted to talk to me was waiting out front. I remember he was standing in the front lawn/grassy area looking a little strange, like almost in shock.

I walked over and asked him with concern, "Sir, is there a problem? What is going on?"

He paused for a moment and replied to me shakingly, "Yeah… Sal decided to leave us."

I did not know what that meant, but the first thing that came to mind was that someone had run away or had been lost. Such as a missing person situation. Another thought that came to mind was that I knew some older people were living in this home, so maybe someone had passed away. I told the man, "Let's take a walk inside and see how I can help." Inside we went.

Once inside, the man and I walked upstairs to the area where the bedrooms were located. As I entered each of them, I was looking for someone laying on the floor, or in the bed. I did not see anything, so I turned to the man and asked him again, "Who lives here?"

He told me, "Me and Sal". I was not sure if they were father and son or roommates.

Since I did not see anyone. I asked, "Where is Sal?"

"He's there…." The man replied.

At that point, I was confused. The man pointed at an old, slatted door with a lift-type latch. A very colonial-looking door with tongue and groves on it. It was very narrow, probably only two feet wide. I then popped up the latch and opened the door slowly.

Right smack in front of me, there was Sal… deceased and hanging with a noose around his neck. I was shocked and was not expecting that! Looking at his back from the shoulders down reminded me of Vietnam, where I had been on two tours of duty and have witnessed all the gruesome horrors of war. This situation had a similar type of weird feel to it. However, I have never seen someone in person who took their own life by hanging. Although I mentioned another hanging incident in a previous story, this one was the first in my career. I'd seen pictures and all that in our old police case files, but I'd never seen anything in person. Remember that I mentioned in a previous story, as a police officer, sometimes, we need to find a little humor in very bad situations? It's kind of like a coping mechanism.

I just stepped back from the body and counted "1, 2, 3, 4, 5, 6, 7, 8, 9, 10." Then I walked away and called on the radio for the sergeant to come to the scene. Fifteen-20 minutes later, Sergeant Al Smith arrived. He was the type of guy who had unique mannerisms about him. He had these hand gestures like the old comedian, W.C. Fields. Smith used to roll his fingers in front of him while talking and had a bit of an odd accentuation of the verbal language. For example, when he arrived and walked up to the scene, he first said to me, "Okay, Jim Boy… What do we got?"

I said, "Sargeant, this is what we got!" pointing upwards.

Very nonchalantly, Smith said twice in a row, "Okay, Jimmmmmy Boy, we gotta get him down…. we gotta get him down." This was the humor I mentioned…Smith talking in the voice that he did and with his mannerisms. I found him funny during that serious moment of gloom when he was not trying to be. He was being himself. He was a great guy.

So, then he said to me, "Jimmmmy... you gotta go up there and get him down." So, up the narrow attic stairs I went. I had to squeeze by and push the body out of the way, which was rubbing up against me, to get to the top of the stairs. I did not want to look at the victim, especially in the face, because the way the rope pulls the skull off the neck puts people in very unnatural positions, as you can imagine. I was not sure if this was the case, but I did not want to find out. After getting by the body, I saw where the rope was tied off at the top of the stairs. I told myself, *"You've seen all kinds of horrific stuff from your past experiences, so just turn around and look at him. Just do it."* When I finally got to the top of the stairs, I turned around and looked at the victim. It was not as bad as I thought it was going to be and did not shock me as much as I thought it would.

The rope was tied to a beam in the ceiling then wrapped around the railing and onto his neck. He must have sat and then dropped down into the stairwell. I undid the rope and let Sgt. Smith know below that I released the victim. I then heard, "Okay, Jimmy Boy, lower him down. Lower him down, Jimmy Boy." That's exactly what I did, and I was chuckling to myself while I did because Sergeant Smith was saying it in the manner that he was saying it. Humor.

We took the victim, moved him into the hallway, put a sheet over him, and called the old man back into the room from outside. He wanted to pay his last respects to Sal. We ended that call by helping the old man get in touch with a funeral home and waited with him until they arrived. We then advised him on the next steps and the process. A sad day for him certainly, and a strange one for us as police officers.

SOUTH SALEM AREA

POPCORN ANYONE?

Location: *72 Loring Avenue*
Coordinates: *42.50028* N, 70.89651* W*

This is a story about a couple of brothers by the last name of Kincade, whom the Lynn Police Department knew very well at the time. One day in Salem, at the Little Peach convenience store (located at the end of Jefferson Avenue and Canal Street), a robbery took place. Two men went in with pistols, stole a bunch of cash and cartons of cigarettes, and left the place. We Detectives received the report and started our investigation. We ended up asking the store manager for the videotape if they had any of the day's activities. Fortunately, they had a camera in a great spot in the store and provided us with a copy of the tape. We brought it back to the station, started watching it, and noticed something helpful.

The clip showed two guys walking in and then just standing there. One bought a pack of cigarettes, and when his arm reached out to give the cashier money, we noticed a significant tattoo on his forearm. After the guy received his change, he left the store. About two hours later, two masked men came in and robbed the store, and lo and behold, there was that same tattoo on the arm! What made this robbery a little humorous was that behind the cashier's counter was this big, green neon sign that said, "YOU ARE BEING VIDEOTAPED." Apparently, they did not see that sign!

After watching the three or so hours of videotape, we made some calls to the Detective offices of the other surrounding police departments, asking if they recognized anybody who had these tattoos. Sure enough, the

Lynn Police Department said, those are the Kincade brothers! We ended up getting a warrant, connected with the Lynn Police, and raided their home to arrest them. They lived on Essex Street in Lynn in a three-family unit house on the second floor. After apprehending them, we took them back to the Salem Police Department for questioning.

Here is the great part of the story. After they sat down in our Detective's office, we handed them a bag of popcorn that we purchased specially for this occasion. We did not say a word when we did it. Just stared at them in complete silence. They then looked at us aloofly like they did not know what to think.

Then the brothers both asked, "What the hell are you giving us a bag of popcorn for?"

We said, "Well, we have a hit movie that you just have to watch!"

We pulled up the old TV on wheels and played the videotape. Of course, they saw themselves on the video, and we just sat there smiling. They just kind of hung their heads and knew they were caught. We played it beautifully, and they ended up being charged with armed robbery.

THE HENRY HILLARD CASE

Location: *466 Loring Avenue; Various*

Coordinates: *42.48944* N, 70.89748* W*

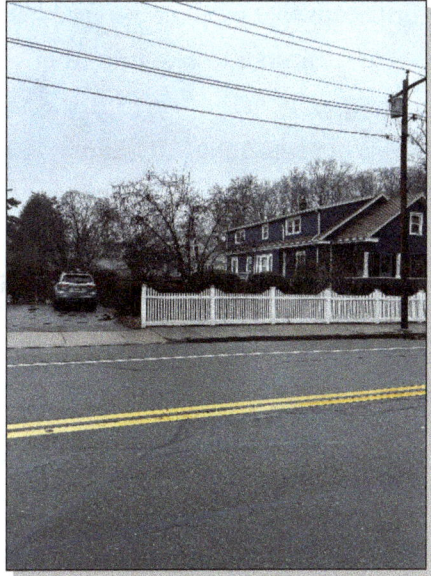

Back in the seventies, Salem dealt with a brutal serial rapist. The first victim that was reported to Salem Police was a 12-year-old girl who was walking down Lafayette Street, coming from a friend's house. She reported that a man came up from behind her, put a knife to her throat, and pulled her into some bushes on Leavitt Street. He wanted some money, so he took like the $2 that she had on her. He then proceeded to sexually assault her and told her that if she said anything, he was going to find her again and kill her. Then he ran off. By the way, this attack occurred late at night, around one or two o'clock in the morning.

Detective Mark Riley was the initial investigator on that case and assault. Then, about a week or so later, we had another assault off of Lafayette Street, where a woman was walking up Holly Street. She reported that a black man came up behind her, held a knife to her throat, and said that he was going to kill her. She did not comply with his demands, so he sexually assaulted her. One of the things that happened in this particular case was that she had on a pair of semi-high-heeled shoes. Inside the shoes, there was a metal bar in the arch area that kept the shoe in its position. Apparently, it was loose inside of her shoe. The woman took the piece out, and she stabbed him in the thigh with the metal piece. He then ran off and left her behind. He did not complete his assault on this woman.

One evening, I was at home, on Oak View Avenue in Salem, with my wife at the time. It was summertime, and she was going out with her girlfriends that evening. I stayed behind. As I was lying in bed reading, I heard a car door close out in front of my house. I thought it was my wife coming home at that time, but she never came into the house. So obviously, it was not her. About 10 minutes later, I got a phone call from the station, and it was my partner, Dick Urbanowicz. He said to me, "Jim, you gotta come in. Henry struck again." This person named Henry Hillard was a suspect of ours, but we could never tie him directly to any of the assaults.

I said, "You have to be kidding me. Again?"

"There's another thing, Jim" Dick said.

"What's that?" I answered.

Dick said, "The assault happened right in your backyard."

Well, that caught me totally by surprise! The assault really did not happen exactly in my backyard but did occur in two of my adjacent neighbors' backyards. I'll explain that now.

A young girl was walking home from Beverly. She'd had a fight with a boyfriend and was walking up Loring Avenue. Henry Hillard was driving up Loring Avenue and saw the girl walking alone. He pulled onto Oak View Avenue, parked his vehicle, and entered my next-door neighbor's backyard. The home was right on the corner of Loring and Oakview. When Henry was in the backyard, he stepped into the homeowner's garden. An item of noteworthiness was that my neighbor had a specific fertilizer formula he used in his garden. This was important, so remember that point.

Henry was wearing sandals at this particular time and made footprints in the soft soil in the garden. When the woman got up to the area where Henry was, he jumped over the fence and waited in some bushes. When the girl got close to him, he leapt out at her, put a knife to her throat, and dragged her down onto the grass.

Henry proceeded to drag her into my other neighbor's yard, which was diagonal from the house that I lived in, threw her down onto the driveway, and told her to take her clothes off. She complied because she was at knifepoint. It was reported later that Henry demanded oral sex.

This woman, a gal from Lynn, was street-smart. She told him, "I have a venereal disease, so I can't." Henry said, "I don't care." So, she started to perform that act, and just when she was doing that, the man who lived in that house pulled into the driveway. Henry got scared and ran out of the yard onto Loring Avenue, then back onto my street, Oakview Avenue. He then got into the car and drove away. That was the car door closing that I heard. Well, Henry was not finished with his night.

He went off to Marblehead, driving on Lafayette Street, and saw another girl walking alone where the Old Age Center in Marblehead is located today. In the back of that area was all woods at the time. Henry parked his car right in the main driveway of this random house. He was brazen his actions because he thought no one was home. Again, like his past assaults, he jumped out of the car when this girl was walking close, ran up to her, and put the knife to her throat. Again, he said he was going to kill her if she did not do what he wanted. He dragged her into some bushes, which is now the entrance to the new high school area in the present day and started assaulting her. This time, though, there were some young kids who were probably 10 or 12 years old riding their bicycles in the area, and they heard all this commotion in the bushes. They screamed, "Hey, what's going on in there?!" Henry stopped, panicked, and ran through the woods. He dropped his knife and came out by the post office in Marblehead. He then doubled back out onto Lafayette Street.

As Henry turned the corner, a young kid from Middleton was there. He was like 14 or 15 years old, and he was into building automobiles. The kid was in Marblehead at that time to see if he could purchase a radiator for a car he was building. Henry walked by him and said, "Hey, man, how you doing?" The kid did not know why he even talked to him, but he watched him get into his car, which was later described as a green 1976 Pontiac LeMans with dice hanging in the mirror. The car also had mag wheels. The kid described the car perfectly, which was important because, earlier in the day, another Salem Detective, Billy Jennings, was working a detail up on Highland Avenue at the Heartland Food Store and saw Henry with his girlfriend in that specific car. That was a connection that we needed to tie him to these assaults.

Amazingly, Henry was not through with his activities that night. He left Marblehead and drove by that kid twice. He went towards downtown Marblehead, must have got disoriented, turned around, drove back by the kid, and headed towards Swampscott. While he was going through Swampscott, a young lady, who was recovering from a car accident, was taking a nightly walk to get the blood moving. She was wearing a neck brace to keep her head steady. Henry pulled up his car a little way past her and got out. Again, it was the same assault in the same manner. He assaulted her on a lawn on Humphrey Street for several minutes. He took her license from her and, this time, said he would kill her and her family if she ever said anything, noting that he knew where she lived.

Well, he was finally done for the night. He drove home to Lynn. The next day, we applied for and received an emergency arrest warrant from the judge. We immediately went to his residence in Lynn and arrested him. He struggled with us in the hallway, but we subdued him quickly and took him into custody. We also had a search warrant for clothing that the victims described during those ordeals. We took him to the Lynn Police Station but needed to transport him to Salem.

Henry wouldn't come out of the cell! A bunch of us were standing around waiting for him to come out, and he kept refusing. He kept saying that we were going to beat him up and all that. We assured him that we were not, and yet he still would not exit. We needed to transport him, so I took it upon myself to step into the cell, stood up to him closely, and said, "Look, you're either going to have come out of the cell on your own, or we're going to have to use force to remove you." Well, he ended up walking out of the cell, and we handcuffed him. We took him back to the Salem Police Station.

After Henry was arrested, we submitted all our evidence to the State Crime Lab for analysis. We also set up a photo ID session with Henry. Danvers Police Department was the newest police department at the time, and they had a room with a one-way mirror. The victims were all brought into that particular spot to view a line-up. Henry, along with several other individuals, including Henry's brother and a couple of police officers from different departments, were in the lineup. I believe there were six individuals in the lineup. Henry was visually picked out by our victim and was also picked out unanimously by all the other victims because of his voice. We had everyone in the lineup say the words that Henry said during the time of the assault on the girls from Swampscott.

When the analysis came back from the State Police crime lab, the microscopic samples of the sandals that we had acquired through the search warrant matched the microscopic samples from my next-door neighbor's garden! Remember that I told you about the special fertilizer concoction? We also took plaster casts of the footprints in the garden at the time and matched those up to the sandals Henry was wearing at the time of that attack.

During our investigation, we learned that Henry 's girlfriend said it was unusual for him to come home and not want to have intercourse. So that helped verify what he was doing that night. He'd had enough sexual activity. More circumstantial evidence.

This case went to trial, and the evidence was overwhelming. Henry ended up pleading guilty to these charges, and he was given two life sentences for aggravated sexual assault. These were very heinous crimes, so the sentence was justified. A dangerous guy was off the street, thanks to the efforts of many.

Henry was a football player at a known college in Massachusetts. The college had thrown him out of school because of a sexual assault that he was involved in while he was on campus. There was never any formal documentation about that, unfortunately. Looking back, one interesting thing about this case was that Henry initially said he was not involved in any of the incidents on that particular night. He said he was over in Lynn at the General Electric Plant, picking up his dad, who was getting off a shift at 11 PM. When we spoke with Henry 's father, he said his son was never there to pick him up. He knew that his son was a very dangerous individual, and he ended up offering to be a witness against Henry if he did go to trial.

This case was very satisfying to the Salem Detectives at-large, to the Massachusetts State Police who were involved, to me personally, and especially to the victims.

BOSTON STREET AREA

A CLOSE CALL AT THE OLD FLYNN TANNERY

Location: 70 Boston Street
Coordinates: 42.52014* N, 70.91035* W

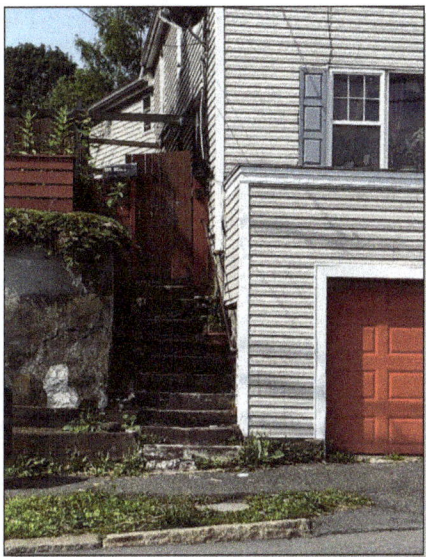

Several years ago, I was working patrol with another officer named Babe Little. Babe was a character, but he was one of the guys in the police department that I also looked up to. He talked in mumbles, and you did not understand what he was saying most of the time. However, when he wanted to say something important, he did say it very clearly. For the most part though, he was mumbling.

Anyways, he and I were working in the "3-Car," which covered the Highland Avenue and the Boston Street area of town. We were driving down from Essex Street and then down Boston Street towards Bridge Street. We looked up and saw flames coming out of the side of the Flynn Tannery building! At the time, Flynn Tannery was located on Boston Street in Salem. Babe and I said to each other, "Oh my God, that's a hell of a fire going on right there!" It was like one or two o'clock in the morning. Thank goodness it was a quiet time for traffic.

Babe and I drove up towards Grove Street, which is on the top of Boston Street, where a set of streetlights was located. Those streetlights are still there in the same place today. We blocked off the road from that side with our cruiser, turned on the flashing lights, and immediately called for another cruiser to block off the other side of the road down near Bridge Street (near where Dunkin Donuts is now located). We then called the Salem Fire Department, and they were already in the process of responding. In the meantime, I was standing in the middle of Boston Street, right across from the Tannery building, pretty much on the double yellow line strip. The flames were going high at that point, and the smoke was intense. That building was made of a lot of dry wood with chemicals soaked into it. Also, they used to keep piles of leather and pallets of chemicals inside of the building. This was not a recipe for safety, as this area of Salem has been known for tanneries and tannery fires over the last hundred years. It was not OSHA compliant by today's standards to say the least!

Suddenly, I heard this rumble inside the building. It was like a force of energy that started to protrude outward. As I looked up at the building again, the whole side of it started to come down. The outside brick wall was toppling towards me! There were several cars that were parked right up against the curb in the path of destruction and when the wall came down, it was like slow motion. If I did not move, I was going be buried under a rubble of bricks and then whatever else there was.

I ran as fast as I could away from the collapse and up an old set of stairs across the street. You can see those stairs in the picture as they are still there today. The bricks smashed down onto Boston Street, crushing those parked cars in its path. The embers of the bricks flying in the air hit me in the back. It was like getting peppered with shotgun pellets. It was a close call, but I managed to pull through on that one. We never really did find out what happened at the Flynn Tannery and what/who caused the fire. Fortunately, there were no fatalities as no one was in the building at the time that late at night.

Babe and I stuck around until the fire was out and our shift ended. When the other officers started the morning shift, it was one of the best reliefs I have ever had.

STORIES OF INTEREST

PETER WRIGHTMAN

What got me on my path to pursuing a police career to help people was one that was internal to me. Helping people is my passion, and I carry the philosophy, "If I'm able to help, I will." This philosophy started I'm sure because of a traumatic event that occurred way back when I was ten years old in 1959. I was swimming with a bunch of friends up at Brown's Pond in Peabody. One of my friends that I was with was a boy by the name of Peter Wrightman. He was a classmate of mine. Now, if you looked at Brown's Pond from a bird's eye view, it has the shape of a lightbulb. Bay State Road runs perpendicular to the narrow end of the light bulb shape. Today, there isn't a beach there, but back then, there was. This is where Peter was swimming.

Peter was about 40 yards out from the shoreline, swimming across. At the same time, a fire broke out at a local clam shack-type restaurant nearby, and the fire engines arrived. I was on the shoreline watching and listening to the action. All my other buddies ran up to see the action. I was alone on the beach, and as I turned around, I saw Peter about halfway across the pond. Suddenly, he got cramped up and started to yell out for help. Being alone, I yelled at this woman and hysterically asked if she could help my friend and that he was in trouble. She says, "I really don't know how to swim." I decided I needed to swim out to him and try to help him.

I ran down, jumped in the water, and swam to Peter as fast as possible. When I reached him, he was extremely panicked, and he latched onto me very aggressively. The next thing I knew, both of us were underwater, sinking to the bottom. He was grabbing onto and holding me with such a strong clutch. I was trying to save him by calming him down, but he wouldn't let me. We both sank to the bottom. It was dark down there, and I could feel the pond grass around my feet. We were probably down there eight or ten feet. I could see his face in front of me with the bubbles coming out of his mouth, yelling. I thought to myself, I don't want to die because I've heard about people trying to save other people, and then both people ended up dying.

I had to fight Peter off to go up to the surface and get some air. I swam up and saw the sun shining through the water up above. When I reached the surface, I broke through the water, took a deep breath, and started yelling for help. Fortunately, two teenage boys heard and came running down, and they swam out. I yelled to them, "He's right down here. He is right down here!" The bigger teens were able to get him out and bring him back to the beach. The Peabody Fire Department came down and applied oxygen to him. They then took him away in an ambulance. Peter passed away. He never made it, and I was the last person to touch and see Peter alive. That experience left a significant imprint on my life. It was traumatic, for sure.

On the day of his funeral, Peter's family asked me to ride in the limousine with them. After the funeral was over, they took me to Peter's house, which was a beautiful house in a nice neighborhood. His father took me up to his bedroom where he had little model airplanes hanging from the ceiling. I came from a poor background and did not really have that much. I never had a brand-new bike or anything like that. Peter Wrightman's father offered me his new bicycle and told me he wanted me to have it. They gave me a ride back home, and I had him drop me off a couple of streets away from my house because I was embarrassed. I felt bad when I thought about being in Peter's room with his father. It was such a nice room for a boy who was no longer there.

Today, when I look back to when I was a boy that day, I think about how I wish I had been able to help Peter more than I could have. However, I was ten years old and did not have the strength or the swimming training to save him. No one my age would have been able to. So, as the years went by and I became a police officer in 1974, I was already prebuilt with a passion for helping people. I wanted to ensure I could give everything I had to help others. Being a police offer was the perfect job to do just that.

Several years later, a new Beverly Bridge was built when I was working as a Detective. A man decided to take his own life by jumping off the center of the bridge, which was about 60 or so feet high. This was in the wintertime, right around February, and it was the early 1990s. I had two college interns with me at the time of investigating the suicide. The interns and I drove down to Dead Horse Beach down at the Salem Willows Park, where this gentleman's body had floated up on shore. I walked down the sand to where this deceased person was to inspect. When I got to the body, I went through his pockets to see if I could find out who he was. When I returned to the car, the two interns asked me, "How can you do that? How can you just touch a dead body like that and go into their pockets?" I said, "Hey, this person is somebody's father, brother, or uncle. We must find out who he is and let the relatives know what happened to him." We drove back to the police station together, and on the way, I told the interns the story of my childhood experience with Peter Wrightman.

Once in the office, I sat at another detective's desk to jot down some notes while they were fresh in my mind. In his cubicle, this detective had a habit of putting up funny and humorous obituaries about people. Like for instance, if a guy were a trash collector, it would say in the obituary, "…so and so was a collector of treasures and artifacts." However, I was not looking at the humorous ones; I was reading another obituary where the name of the deceased person had a couple of "T"s in their last name, like "Worttman" or something like that. So, as I'm reading through this, the obituary said, "pre-deceased by Peter Wrightman." Just then, the hairs stood up on the back of my neck. Seeing that and telling these two students about Peter Wrightman about half an hour earlier was a very weird coincidence.

Peter Wrightman's sister was listed as a relative of this person. I looked her up, gave her a telephone call, and told her about Peter Wrightman's story. She had no remembering of her brother's death at all. She was just a young toddler when that happened. She said the only one who would remember that was their father, who lived in Maine. I hesitated to get in touch with him to not churn up old trauma. All these events seem to tie together. It was a very weird experience for me.

Switching gears on you now and fast-forwarding into the future even more, one of the Salem police officers who had retired from the police department was a gentleman by the name of Charles Bergman. They called him "Chucky" Bergman. Chucky said to me one day that he, unfortunately, had the ability to reach beyond this realm and get in contact with deceased individuals. Of course, I was a little skeptical about that. However, we had another Salem Police officer who had a child who was murdered, sadly. One day, years after the murder, Chucky caught this police officer in the corridor and said something to him that made his face turn white.

A few weeks earlier, that police officer was up on a high ladder painting the peak of his house. Just then, the officer's deceased daughter appeared to him as a vision almost to comfort him as he found himself in this dangerous situation up so high. He climbed back down the ladder, sat at the foundation of his house, and pondered what he had just seen. The officer had never told anybody about his vision. So, the day Chucky caught the officer in the corridor, he told him that he knew that he saw his daughter when he was up on the ladder. He reconfirmed that she was there to protect and comfort him. Goosebumps...

One day, many years later, after Chucky and I both retired, I picked up the phone and called him. I said, "Chuck, I've got a situation I'd like to discuss. I'd like to know about this little boy that died." I never told him anything about Peter Wrightman and the situation that I was in when I was ten years old back in 1959. I investigated several child sexual abuse cases over a period of 25 years, so I thought Chuck figured I was talking about one of those cases where someone had passed away. Chuck said to me, "Call me next week in the afternoon, and we can talk about it." As I said, Chuck was retired at this point and was doing these psychic sorts of readings for people.

The following week, I called him back and we started to chat. I asked Chuck what he wanted me to do regarding this story.

He said, "I want you to have an open mind and just relax." I was lying in my bedroom on the bed while on the phone, totally relaxed.

"Okay, I've got an open mind, and I'm relaxed, Chuck" I replied.

Chuck paused for a moment, and there was silence on the call. Then he told me to wait a minute. Another pause. Then he said, "Jim, I see small planes." Now, I knew a friend who had a small passenger plane and I used to fly down to Nantucket with him. I had made the trip with him several times, and that was the only small plane I could think of.

Then I thought about it again and said to Chuck, "I know that this 10-year-old boy had small planes hanging from the ceiling in his room."

Suddenly, Chuck said to me, "Jim, I see him. I see this boy. He is smiling. He is jumping up and down. He is so happy you remember the planes he had hanging in his room. Let me see what else he is saying." Chuck then told me that he saw the boy grabbing at me, clutching at me, and trying to hold me.

I said, "Chuck, you're not going to believe this, but that was exactly what happened in this situation. Chuck, I want to know how he feels about how I reacted to the situation that day."

Chuck pondered a minute, then responded, "I see a seal. He made a banging sound too. I see a seal, like a....... like a seal or a stamp."

"I have no idea what that means or what it is," I said.

Then Chuck said, "It's a stamp of approval." That comment made me feel really good that Peter Wrightman was giving me the stamp of approval for my efforts that day, trying to save him. Then Chuck said to me, "he's been watching you, watching over you your whole life." I thought that was profound because I had joined the Marine Corps out of high school, did two tours in Vietnam, and had come so close to dying so many times. I always thought it was the little scapular I carried around from my first communion. I still carry that scapular around to this day, but knowing now that Peter Wrightman was the one who was watching over me all these years and still is. It gives me a real sense of peace.

THE WICCAN EXPERIENCE

Location: *12 Pope Street*
Coordinates: *42.51695* N, 70.90818* W*

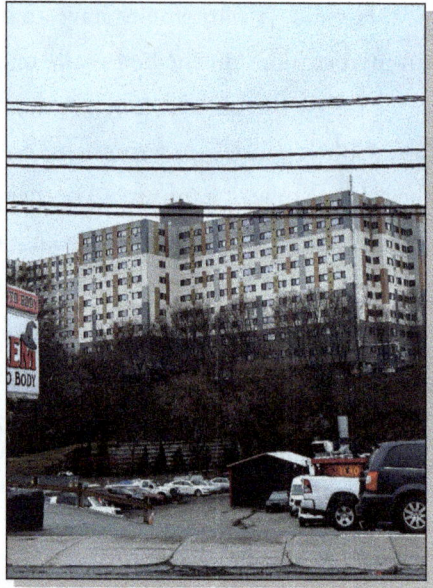

Several years ago in February, a young couple was living at the apartments in Salem. There were, and still are, two big apartment buildings on Pope Street. The gentleman who lived in the apartment was wheelchair bound and was married to this girl. The reason that he was confined to a wheelchair was because a few years before that, he was up in New Hampshire, and he attempted to commit suicide. He planned on hanging himself in the woods in a ravine. He hung the rope over a tree, put the noose around his neck, and flung himself out over the edge. The rope gave away, and he fell onto some rocks several feet below, shattering his spine. He was paralyzed from the waist down. His name was Neil, and he was married to this woman, Gabrielle.

Gabrielle and Neil's relationship was a tumultuous one. Through many hardships, they ended up having a baby through artificial insemination. One day Neil came into the police department and wanted to report his wife missing. Interestingly, there was a two-week period when he waited from when she went missing to when he reported her missing to the police. We took the case on as something seemed off.

The first thing we did in the investigation was to speak to neighbors living in the same building adjacent to his apartment. One of the neighbors told us that they heard two people screaming and yelling from Neil's apartment. Then suddenly, there was a lot of banging, and she was yelling, "Leave me alone" and all that. It sounded like a very confusing situation. Another neighbor living next to them stated that the plumbing started to back up too. We found this a little suspicious because the plumbing connected directly to Neil's and Gabrielle's apartment. Were things being flushed down the toilet or garbage disposal to rid them? Something was not adding up for us. We figured the banging that the neighbors heard might've been him beating her or something like that. What was also odd about her being missing was that she left her winter coat behind in the closet, and it was the middle of February. Do people leave without their jackets? Likely not. Last, we noticed that her pocketbook was still there. We had gotten word that she had a paycheck from her job which was waiting for her to be picked up. She never picked up the check.

Neil told us that Gabrielle probably ran off with a trucker that was waiting for her outside. Again, this sounded odd, so we looked a little further. We obtained a search warrant to go to their apartment and look for human blood. We thought that maybe he had beat her up, cut her body up, and deposited her down the trash chute of the building. We considered this a possibility because he was seen on video wheeling his wheelchair with two large bags going from one building where he lived to the next. He was then seen depositing these bags down the trash chute. It was Martin Luther King Day weekend, and we searched to see if there was trash in the huge bins. Unfortunately, the trash had already been picked up, and we did not know where the final destination was. It was something we had to figure out.

In the meantime, we asked Neil if he would come in and take a polygraph test regarding his missing wife. He refused, saying he was on several medications, and he did not think that the test results would be accurate. We figured he knew the results would not come out in his favor anyway. At that time, we put the word out to the other police departments via an All-Points bulletin to start looking for Gabrielle. One of the Salem police officers in charge at the time stepped up and said that he belonged to the Wiccan community. This was surprising. Then he then told us that he ran this situation by the local witch of Salem and that she could tell us where the body might be.

Right after he told us this update, he then turned to me and asked if I would meet with her at her house with him. He explained that she would go into a trance and then proceed to tell us where the body was located. Obviously, I was skeptical, but as a police officer, one cannot leave any stone unturned. Also, I wanted to let the officer in charge save face with the local witch. Another reason was a little bit of defense, as I could not say no because people could have questioned later why our office did not turn over every proverbial stone.

I went down with this captain to the local witch's house, and we all sat in her kitchen. She then 'supposedly' put herself into a trance. She did some grunting and groaning, then flickered her eyes a bit and then shook her body around. When she snapped out of it, she stated that she thought Gabrielle was off Mount Washington Road in New Hampshire, down a ravine. Well, this was the middle of February, and Mount Washington Road is closed in February. Realistically, how could have Gabrielle's body been laid there at that time of the year? When springtime rolled around, we did go up there when everything thawed out. We conducted a thorough search of the ravines that were off Mount Washington Road and found nothing. That was my experience with the local witch.

Massachusetts State Police trooper Mitch Canvendish and I were involved in this case, as was my Salem colleague Conrad Prosniewski, who was a Detective at the time. Conrad was doing some background checking and research himself. He received an outside tip regarding a pornographic website that had a female picture that looked awfully like the alleged victim, Gabrielle. We followed up on this, and it was not Gabrielle. It was some woman from Canada. We put out an "all-points" bulletin regarding social security numbers to see if hers was used anywhere in the United States, to no avail -- another dead end.

Years later, we got in touch with their once little baby, now a grown man. We asked to obtain his DNA samples to see if we could match his

DNA with his mother's. He gave his approval, and we put his DNA into the database in case some remains were found somewhere that we could match up with. Nothing… another dead end. To close this story out, this case has yet to be solved and it remains to this day a cold case. We have not heard anything about this case since my retirement, and hopefully, it will be solved someday.

MEDIA RELATIONSHIPS THEN AND NOW

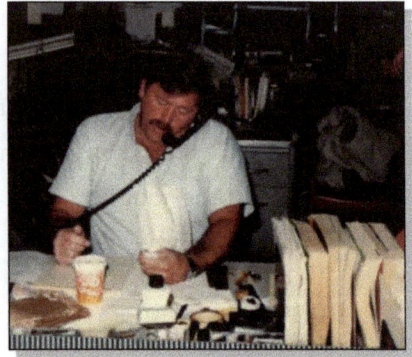

Working as a police officer from the 1970s through the 1990s was certainly a different time than today in many respects. One of those differences is the saturation and prevalence of the media. Today's police officers, locally, state, and federally, are subject to more oversight and scrutiny than in prior year's past. This is for the better and the worse. The media is your friend, but it can also be your adversary. In the past, there have been situations where we would have liked a comment to stay off the record, and unfortunately, it came out in the media afterwards. So, we learned how to try and build some trust with individual reporters. Those relationships were built over time and through experiences together.

I remember a particular case where a woman who was despondent and not mentally together ended up falling out of an apartment window and died. I responded to the scene to investigate how this could have occurred. There was also a reporter on the scene who was asking questions about this incident. I answered a few of the questions, and his replies weren't very sensitive. It was like he acted differently to get some sort of response from me and was playing my comments off as no big deal. I asked him not to make a big splash in the news about it. The next day, in the newspaper in big, capital-lettered, bold one-inch letters was a headline that said, "WOMAN LEAPS TO HER DEATH." I remember I was mortified because I really felt bad for the family, and we really did not know if she leapt or just fell until we investigated further.

The next day, I called that reporter and told him I did not appreciate his remarks in the paper. It was a tragic occurrence, and it was framed in such an insensitive and perhaps not truthful way.

He responded to me, "Well, Jim, you know, it's a story that people want to hear."

I said, "Yeah, but they did not need it to hear in the manner that you presented it. Also, it could have been on page four in the bottom left-hand column of the paper. Instead, you had a front-page feature story with one-inch bold letters. That was not the way to be sensitive to the person's family." That was not a great experience with the media.

However, on the other hand, we had a reporter from the Boston Herald who worked with us. He used to accompany us on drug raids and other situations where photography was a big part of the evidence. The Herald photographer took "action shots" of suspects being arrested. It helped the police with using these pictures when the DA used some of them for photos in court. That man was a very good investigative reporter and photographer. He may still be working in today's market now. I'm not sure. I will say though, that that reporter presented things in the way they should...factual and unbiased as much as possible. The manner he reported was in true detail without exploiting anybody's feelings or the tragedy itself.

Back in the 1970s through the 1990s, there was no social media, internet, and cell phones with cameras. Media outlets were really limited to TV, radio, and print. Information sharing and transfer happened much more slowly. Today, info sharing is instantaneous, and everyone is really a "reporter" today, having access to a camera and posting on some social media site. Every incident is filmed and posted for the world to see many times without context or a complete video. Snippets of a video can warp viewpoints. Since info transfer happens so rapidly, it makes the job of a police officer very difficult in today's environment. It will be interesting to see how the relationship between the media, everyday citizens filming with their phones, constitutional "auditors," and the police grows closer or further apart over the next decade or so -- such a complex relationship today versus the simplicity back in the day.

FIREARMS AND HIGH-SPEED CHASES

Boston Street Roadblock

Early in my patrol career in 1976, I was involved in a situation where a high-speed chase from out-of-state ended with some gunfire in Salem. Here is how this situation went down. There was a guy from New Hampshire who was involved in a shooting up north over the border and was coming down reportedly to Salem. We received some information that he was driving through Peabody Square and had a rifle with him. As he drove through Peabody Square and headed towards Boston Street into Salem, we set up a roadblock at the top of Boston and Essex Street. At the corner of those two streets was a Super Sub at the time. As that car was coming up the hill, we were in position with our pistols out and leaning over our cruisers. We were anxiously waiting for this individual to come up the street in his vehicle.

The individual stopped his car, probably 50 yards away from us, and got out of his vehicle. He had a rifle in his hand and proceeded to point our way. Several of the officers opened fire on him. One of the Patrolmen struck the bad guy in the neck. I did not feel any need to shoot because other people were firing away. What I did do when the firing was over was run over to the bad guy as he fell into a snowbank on the side of the road to render medical aid. Blood was pouring from his neck, and I tried to stem the flow of bleeding by putting some direct pressure on the wound. The other officers ended up calling an ambulance. The bad guy survived the gunshot. Soon after that, he was convicted in court for many charges.

Yellow Station Wagon

There was another time when Dick Urbanowicz and I were riding in our patrol car down the Point area of Salem. As we turned from Congress Street onto Palmer Street in our yellow station wagon police cruiser, (Yes, it was a yellow station wagon at the time!) we heard this bang on the back of our vehicle. Someone had taken a shot at our cruiser with a pellet gun and shattered the back window. We never did find out who the individual was, but it certainly put us on notice to stay more vigilant during our patrol sessions.

Gloucester Joy Ride

Here was another time that I probably shouldn't write about, but I will. On two occasions, I was involved in some automobile chases. One of them was down the Willows while on patrol. A car came speeding out of one of the parking lots, and we started to give chase. The vehicle went through Salem into Beverly along Route 127 into the Beverly Farms area, and we were right behind him. Beverly Police tried to set up some quick roadblocks, but the vehicle just drove up onto the sidewalks and went around them. We did the same thing.

The bad guy who was driving that car took one of the side streets that led out from Route 127 onto Route 128 North. We ended up still pursuing this vehicle on 128, and we pulled up alongside the vehicle. I was the passenger in the cruiser while my partner was driving. I instructed him to pull up alongside the vehicle as best he could. Then, I took out my service revolver and took several shots at the rear left tire of the vehicle. The tire popped, and the vehicle went off the side of the road. We were then in the Gloucester area and discovered that the bad guy lived there. He ended up jumping out of the car and disappeared into the darkness of the woods.

The Gloucester Police Department knew who this guy was because he loved to be chased by the cops! Apparently, he had set up this whole scenario in advance. When the bad guy went home to his residence in Gloucester, the police were there waiting for him. He was all cut up from tree branches and bushes from running through the woods on his way back.

Bridge Street

Dick Urbanowicz and I were on patrol one early morning, around 3 AM, and we ended up in pursuit of a car. It was so long ago that I forget the actual reason we ended up chasing this vehicle. Anyway, we were pursuing it outbound on Bridge Street towards Beverly. This was before the current bridge was built. Back then, it was a two-lane bridge; some of the old pilings and ruins are still there today. I knew this was a heavy residential area, but I asked my partner to pull up as close as he could to the rear of that car. Once Dick got close enough, I took two or three shots at the rear tire to try and stop it.

Shooting at a moving target like that was not easy, and I did not hit the tires. We continued the pursuit over the old Beverly Bridge, and we notified the Beverly Police Department that we were in pursuit of this vehicle. They had a police officer patrolling on the other side conveniently, so they immediately set up a one-car roadblock for us. That ended that pursuit quickly.

Another Discharge

There was another instance where I discharged my firearm, which, by today's standards, would be an illegal maneuver. Here is the story. I dated this woman many years ago, and at that time she had bought a brand-new Ford Mustang. I lived in a big high-rise apartment off Loring Avenue in Salem, called Loring Towers. She and I were coming out of my apartment as I went in for my midnight shift. Quickly we noticed that somebody was in her new Mustang trying to steal it! They tried to hotwire the car hoping to get it out of the parking space. I ran over with my badge and gun and confronted them. Immediately, they jumped out of her car, jumped into their own vehicle, and started driving off.

At this point, I grabbed ahold of their driver's side door, and they dragged me along for 10 or 15 feet in the parking lot, and then I had to let go. I did get the license plate number, so when I went into the station for a roll call, I had that license plate number transmitted to other police departments. It turned out to be registered to a person in Lynn.

No sooner than we had our roll call, we then went out on patrol. At the time, Salem Police had just purchased these new, souped-up police interceptors with high-powered engines. My partner and I just happened to be using one of those new cruisers that night. As we started our 8-hour shift, we got a radio call that the Peabody Police Department was pursuing a car, and the vehicle was coming up Marlboro Road. It was going to intersect onto Highland Avenue in Salem. Dick Urbanowicz and I jumped in our cruiser, and we zoomed over with our sirens and lights flashing to that area where Tri-City Sales used to be.

Just as we approached the intersection, that vehicle flew out from Marlboro Road onto Highland Avenue and was heading towards Lynn. We pursued the vehicle up to an area where Rich's Department Store was at the time. That vehicle pulled into the parking lot, and the two individuals jumped out and abandoned their ride. They started running up the side of a hill into a bunch of trees and bushes.

We began to pursue them on foot, shouting for them to stop, but they kept going. Dick and I took out our service revolvers and fired a couple of shots over their head because we knew that there was nothing behind them except the woods. There was a Boy or Girl Scout camp that was located in the area, but it was not occupied at the time. We ended up catching up with the two guys and apprehending them. Dick and I felt pretty good about it because they were two guys in their early 20's and we were a couple of older guys who managed to keep up!

We brought them back to the station, and they were charged with attempted motor vehicle theft and property. We gave them all kinds of citations for speeding, etc. Thank God nothing ever came out of that where anybody was hurt. Today, an unjustified discharge, no matter where the shot went, would end up being a big problem for the officer.

There were two other times when I discharged my firearm to euthanize some critically injured animals and other scenarios like that.

Scaring Myself

This is a funny one. Dick Urbanowicz and I were on patrol during the midnight to eight shift doing our local door checking, making sure the businesses were secure and all that stuff. We were on Dodge Street at the rear of 100 Lafayette Street, and we noticed that there was a broken door panel in the rear door. This door led down to a hall where one of the local girl bands used to practice. The "Ellas," I think they were called.

We both crawled through the opening in the door and had our flashlights and guns out as well. It was pitch dark, and Dick and I split up and started going from room to room very slowly. As I turned one of the corners inside, I saw a figure right in front of me with a flashlight as well, and a gun pointed right at me! I panicked for a second, and then I realized it was a large mirror, and was looking at myself with the gun in my hand. I almost shot myself! Dick and I laughed about that one the rest of the night. Regarding the broken panel, there was no breaking and entering. I think someone just kicked it in at some point.

CYANOACRYLATE

Back in 1981, when I became a Detective, I was fortunate enough to work with the Massachusetts State Police at their crime lab in Cambridge, Massachusetts. I trained in both fingerprinting and photography for eighteen weeks. It was a great experience, and it was the foundation of my knowledge which was refined over the years. When I returned to Salem Police, there was a case of armed robbery at the Wendy's up on Highland Avenue. These individuals stormed into the restaurant with a sawed-off shotgun and a pistol, robbed the place, jumped into a car, and left the scene. The very next day, that automobile was found abandoned in Beverly. Later that morning, I drove over to Beverly to do some examining.

Once I got into the car, I noticed a rubber glove on the backseat floor. I put that glove into an evidence bag and took it back to our own crime lab. The lab we had was outfitted with photography development equipment, chemicals, and fish tanks. You may ask yourself, what were fish tanks doing in the crime lab? Here's why. We borrowed a mannequin's hand from a local store and had it in the lab for just this purpose. I turned the rubber glove inside out and fitted it on that hand. Next, it was put inside that empty fish tank next to a little metal hot plate. Before that metal plate heated up, I would put super glue directly on it, and it would give off a whiteish fume (cyanoacrylate) as it heated up. Those fumes end up sticking to the skin oils and other particulate that the latent fingerprint left behind. It was all done within the tank.

There were powders and several other options as well to make the fingerprints visible. However, the process I described above released a chemical called cyanoacrylate within the glue. It makes the print visible but hardens it through some microscopic crystallization of the oils. With regards to fingerprint dust like you see in the movies, a forensic detective can only lift the dusted fingerprint usually just once using that method. With the super glue method, one can lift it more than once. So, in Wendy's case, I lifted a couple of fingerprints off the inside of the rubber glove and ran them through the automatic fingerprint identification system. That database was used by the Massachusetts State Police and the FBI.

Come to find out that the fingerprint tied back to a gang member out of Lynn, Massachusetts. I don't recall the person's name, but we obtained a warrant and arrested him for armed robbery. The forensic tactics used both at crime scenes and back at the lab varied depending on the circumstances. Even back then, we had many tools in the toolbox to deploy. However, the superglue tactic was always a go-to, and I successfully examined several pieces of evidence over the years using that method.

MY THOUGHTS ON SEARCH WARRANTS AND RAIDS BACK IN THE 1970S AND 1980S

There were all sorts of situations we dealt with back in those days with respect to search warrants and raids. The training was not what it is today. Today, the tactical training looks like military-type training that I used to see in the Marine Corps. Back then, we planned as much as possible with informant intelligence, did our own research, and went ahead. When we performed search warrants and raids, the adrenaline pumped! I got excited, and my heart rate used to elevate. The anticipation of the raid and thoughts of something going wrong were sometimes intense. I mean, we all had families and children at home. We did not want to get hurt, but the chance it could happen was part of the job. However, it was a very satisfying feeling when we pulled off a raid without too much variation in the plan. A lot of times, things went okay, but there have been other situations where our lives could have been taken away if we hadn't had some luck on our side.

THE EXTRA MILE FOR
MEANINGFUL SITUATIONS

A few things that bothered me in my police career were abuse to both people (especially children) and animals. It made my blood boil. However, to last in this profession, one would need to find strategies to mentally survive the long haul. The job is not cut out for a lot of people because we see the underbelly of society that is invisible to so many.

There was this one case that really stood out in my mind. There was a couple that was quarreling, and the guy got so upset at a family member or his girlfriend that he picked up their cat and hurled it against the wall several times. The cat ended up dying. We received a call about this incident and the domestic dispute in general. I went over to the house and retrieved the deceased cat. To prove what happened, we had an autopsy performed on the body.

The feline hospital down on Webb Street helped us out. There was a veterinarian there who performed the autopsy and provided us with a formal report afterward. The vet determined that the cat had suffered a broken neck. We then had cause to arrest the man for animal abuse. I returned to the house and collected some cat hairs and fluids off the wall where the cat was allegedly thrown. This was a piece of solid evidence combined with the cat owner's testimony and the autopsy report. The man was sentenced to six months in jail for animal cruelty.

After this was all said and done, it really came down to us looking into the situation as seriously and comprehensively as we could. At the time, I felt going the extra mile of having an autopsy done on this feline helped resolve that situation, but more importantly prevented anything else from happening to a person living in that home. These things can escalate if not addressed immediately.

In the seventies and early eighties, we police officers knew many individuals in the community. The Detectives and Salem PD at-large looked to step up in these situations and do the right thing. We also knew that situations like this got the attention of the media because no one likes stories of animal abuse. I think if we did not do what we did back then, it would not have looked good for the police department. This feline case did make some headway in the news in a positive way for us for the work we did.

LOSING BET

In the mid-1980s, there was a lively, Chinese restaurant/nightclub located up off Highland Avenue. They had bands playing on the weekends, and fights broke out constantly. I wouldn't say the action there was comparable to the Patrick Swayze movie, "Roadhouse," but it was close to it! Anyway, this place had a lot of cash on site, and the manager of this establishment became worried he was going to get robbed when exiting the rear of the building. He had a hunch about some information he had received, so he called Salem PD to help.

So, a small Detective team set up surveillance one weekend over two nights (Friday-Saturday night). There was a Chevrolet dealership that ran adjacent to the rear road of this spot. We had a couple of guys in the parking lot up there, looking down over the scene. However, we needed somebody close in proximity to where the supposed robbery was going to be where the guy walked out the back door. The only spot that was readily available to do that was inside a dumpster out behind a pizza shop next door.

I'm not sure if I lost a Salem PD bet somewhere along the lines, or if my superiors were upset with me, but I was chosen to be inside the dumpster for two nights! I sat inside with a shotgun and curled up in the corner to make sure that I wouldn't be dumped on with tomato sauce and leftover food coming out of the kitchens! Fortunately, I wore a protective jacket and covered my head. When I was in there, I slid the side door open just enough to see the rear door of the Chinese restaurant where the supposed robbery was to take place. It was my job to interfere with it if the robbery happened. I sat there for two nights in the sweltering heat and endured tomato sauce and all sorts of stuff being thrown in. It had as you would say, "an odiferous odor."

You know what? Nothing ever happened. The robbery did not take place -- the things we did.

HALLOWEEN, AND THE HAUNTED HAPPENINGS

Since the 1600s, Salem has been known as the "Witch City." People from around the world travel to Salem just because of that fact. Back in the early '80s, Salem realized that there was an opportunity for the city to reap the financial benefits of having more people come to Salem, especially during the month of October. Hence the birth of "Haunted Happenings." This event originally was just a parade where everybody got together, made some floats, and got into costume. They would start out at Shetland Park and march down Derby Street, up Washington Street, and all the way up to the Common. From what I remember it was quite a nice atmosphere for families and the kids.

Fast forward to the early '90s, the city started to heavily market in the month of October to visitors, and as time went on, it got to be a little bit rowdier in Salem. The people started to show up more and more, and the crowds became much larger. After the first couple of years of growth, the city decided that this was a boom for it financially. Businesses downtown started to bring in revenue, and taxes hit the coffers. Seeing this, the city started advertising even more on the radio, on TV, on billboards, and again, people started to travel in from around the country and around the world. This is when it became somewhat difficult as a Salem Police officer in the '90s as the visiting crowd's behavior turned into long nights of a Mardi Gras type atmosphere.

Small businesses were also springing up left and right. Witchcraft shops, spell shops, horoscope and palm readers, haunted houses, haunted tours, walking tours, bars, and restaurants. The Hawthorne Hotel would have a huge costume party every year, and many folks that live in the older homes area (Chestnut Street, etc.) would have parties amongst themselves. Things really caught on for Salem. Things caught on big time. While there were no problems in the beginning, that was not the case years later.

Remember, these were times pre 9/11 where strategic crowd control, "see something say something," and anti-terrorism was not really a hot focal point. However, here is how we prepared for Haunted Happenings back then. Typically, it would be the Police Chiefs' responsibility. The Chiefs would get together with other Chiefs from surrounding towns and the same for the Captains. Everybody would sit down and try and plan out the strategy for traffic, crowds, and communication.

Traffic was, and still is, a real issue in Salem so the days of October 28th -31st traffic enforcement became critical. We shut down certain streets, detoured traffic to different areas, and set up approved areas to park. It was at that point where the city encouraged public transportation and buses from various strategic points.

With regards to crowd management, everyone was assigned to a geographic sector of the City. During the last four days of October, all vacations were cancelled unless there was some special circumstance. It was all hands-on deck. There was basically no one in the police station because all were out in their sector. We communicated to each other by radio and often integrated with the State Police radio, as they came in to support us. The Sheriff's department, Beverly Police, Peabody Police, Boston Police, and all sorts of specialized units (K9, Bicycle) helped too. When the actual Halloween night came around it was "game-on" for us. Now, pre 9/11, it really was not too bad that night. We had our hands full of people that became violent, and fights started. We also had a few stabbings and shootings, but all that stuff happened outside the downtown area.

On that night, we Salem Detectives dressed in plain clothes to mix in as one of the thousands of people out there. However, we were wearing our brown gun belt underneath, and handcuffs on us as well. One of the things I remember about that night was how much that gun belt weighed after 10-12 hours standing on your feet. Also, my feet, legs, and back hurt too from standing all night. Another memory was a time when the crowds were crazy in the Essex Street Mall. I remember standing there and just observing the crowd with my partner Jim Page and suddenly we saw this one-liter bottle of Coca-Cola flying in the air and hitting one of the pedestrians that was walking. It was almost impossible to see who threw that bottle because the area was packed like a sardine can. We did get lucky and see who did it, however, so we rushed in and arrested that person.

Another memory was when standing against one of the frontages of a business in the Essex Street Mall, this individual came up to me with a mask on. It was like a Jason hockey mask. He stood right in front of me with that mask about two inches away from my face, not saying a word. I knew it was somebody that I either knew, or somebody that I had encountered in my law enforcement duties in the past. In other words, arrested them or one of their relatives. My guard was up and my response to them was, "Okay, you had your fun. Now it's time to move on." This type of behavior happened multiple times throughout the night and 9 out of 10 times that strategy worked to deescalate.

One Halloween night I remember this incident where some out-of-state visitors in their middle 40s drank way too much alcohol. We were in the process of apprehending another individual near them for being out of control and defacing property. The out-of-state woman got in our face and said, "Hey, that's police brutality. What are you guys doing?" We told her just to move on. I remember the wife or girlfriend of another one of the men started yelling at us that we were acting a little too harshly on the individual we were apprehending. We weren't, we were just doing the necessary force to contain the person. However, this woman wouldn't let up, and ramped up getting in our face screaming at us. One of the other Salem Police officers just kind of said to the husband, "you might want to take her and move her somewhere else, because in another minute she will be joining this individual in a cell somewhere." That leads me to a whole other topic of Halloween night... the cells at the police station.

The station had ten cells for regular individuals, four cells for juveniles, and there was this one big holding area that could hold about 30 or 40 people. Halloween night always produced several inebriated people, both male and female who were taken to this one big area. It really was quite a show and just how you would imagine it being! Stinky, throw-up everywhere, people sleeping, yelling, singing, and even dancing.

Post 9/11, the whole atmosphere of Halloween changed, as you can well imagine. Law enforcement looked at things much more intensely. Halloween, and Salem at the time, was a prime target for a terrorist type situation due to the large crowd packed tight all together. Whether it was handguns, a semi-automatic rifle, or bomb, or even just a stink bomb that people used to throw around, we were on a much higher alert. Salem PD obtained numerous grants (likely flowed down from DHS) and combined with the city budget, procured, and installed several cameras around the city that reported back inside the police station's controls room. The control room back then had around 20 to 30 screens that officers could monitor. That was a huge development and advantage for us to try and get out ahead of problems.

Halloween was somewhat enjoyable for us looking at the costumes but was superseded by the stress. We wanted the City of Salem to do well, and for people to have a good time. However, we often we prayed for rain, snow, and cold weather! The less people, the better it was for us. To sum this up, I do not miss one bit those 20 years of living on the edge during Halloween night.

VINTAGE PHOTOS

Speaking to a few kids in the old Salem Police Station

A formal shot back in the late 70s or very early 80s.

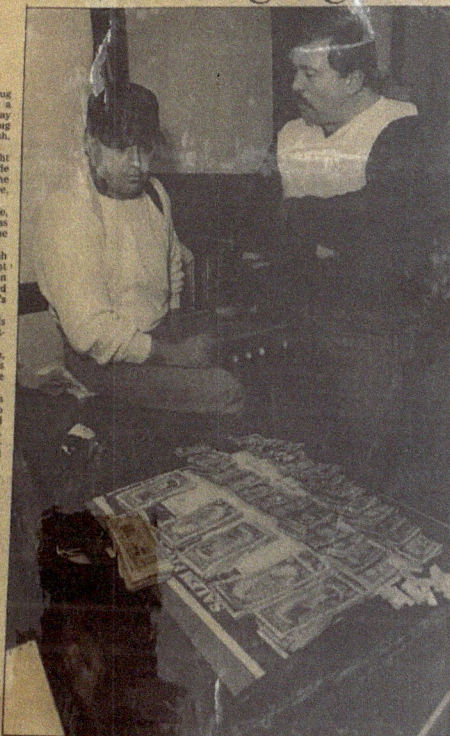

Police nab 3, seize drugs, guns

Salem detectives confiscate $30,000

By GLEN JOHNSON
News Staff

SALEM — After a day of trailing suspected drug users and their suppliers, Salem police raided a Point apartment and another home a half-mile away Wednesday night, arresting three suspected drug dealers and confiscating more than $30,000 in cash, two guns and 40 packets of heroin.

The three are suspected of leading a ring thought to be bringing heroin into the state from Rhode Island and New York City for distribution on the streets of Salem and the rest of the North Shore, according to Det. Sgt. Richard Urbanowicz.

Police arrested Alexis Reynoso, 38, and his wife, Senis Reynoso, 22, both of 42 Park St., as well as Jose R. Delacruz, 39, of 20 Hathorne St., in the Reynoso's third-floor apartment.

Detectives seized more than $3,000 of the cash from a suitcase, a pistol loaded with hollow-point bullets and an unloaded semi-automatic rifle hidden in a closet, plus heroin worth several thousand dollars stashed in a dresser drawer in Reynoso's bedroom, Urbanowicz said.

Police also found an electronic pager and records which they think indicates the group was coordinating a supply ring.

In a raid minutes later at Delacruz's home, detectives seized more than $25,000 in cash, plus more records and telephone numbers thought to be those of suspected drug buyers.

Each of the suspects was charged with possession of a class "A" substance (heroin) with intent to distribute, while Alexis Reynoso also was charged with two counts of illegal possession of firearms. Senis Reynoso was released on personal recognizance Wednesday night, but all were to be arraigned today in Salem District Court, Urbanowicz said.

"I think we got the main supplier down in the (Point) section. Alexis and his wife were big players, but the main man was Delacruz," Urbanowicz said.

Acting on tips from informants, police began a day-long process of watching smaller "runners" pick-up heroin from the Park Street apartment and then distribute the drugs to junkies. Instead of pouncing on the smaller sales, police waited until they saw enough runners return to the Reynoso's apartment, allegedly for a fresh supply of heroin.

"We got the word that there was a guy on the Point (Delacruz, who frequently stayed at the Reynoso's) who could get you anything you wanted, day or night," Urbanowicz said. After getting two search warrants, one for the Park Street apartment and one for Delacruz's Hathorne Street home, detectives raided the buildings.

Detectives brought the electronic pager they seized to police headquarters, turned it on and waited for a call. About 10 p.m. the pager sounded and detectives in an unmarked car went to meet a suspected buyer.

"We had tinted windows on the car and he (the alleged buyer) came right up to the window and

RAIDS
(Continued on page 8)

Salem Police Detectives William L. Jennings, left, and Jim Gauthier look over cash, drugs and weapons seized in a raid early this morning in Salem.

The Salem News (Jonathan M. Whitmore)

Billy Jennings and I discussing the seizure after a successful raid.

The old Salem Police Station's Criminal Investigation Division (CID). In the photo: front to back: Dick Urbanowicz, Conrad Prosniewski, Billy Jennings, Jim Page

CID office from the other direction.

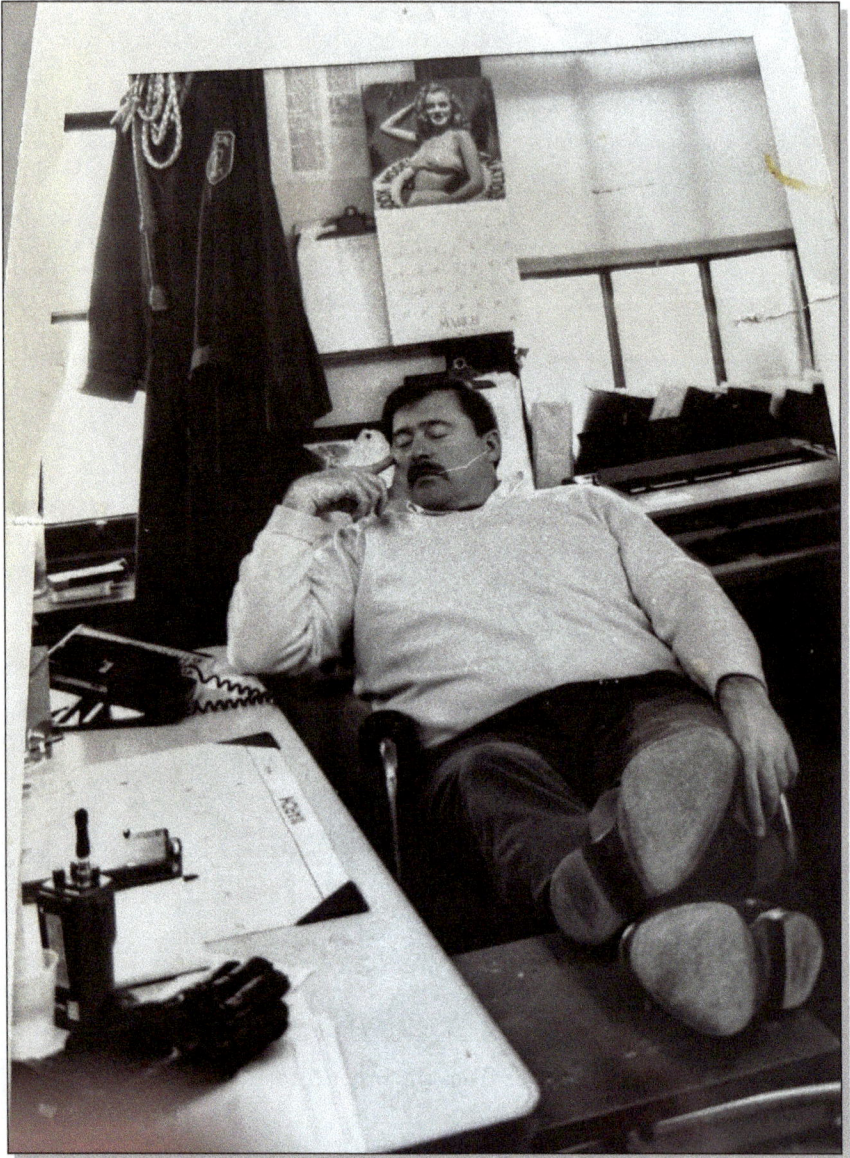

Catching me in a quick power nap from a long night
before, or in deep thought about a case

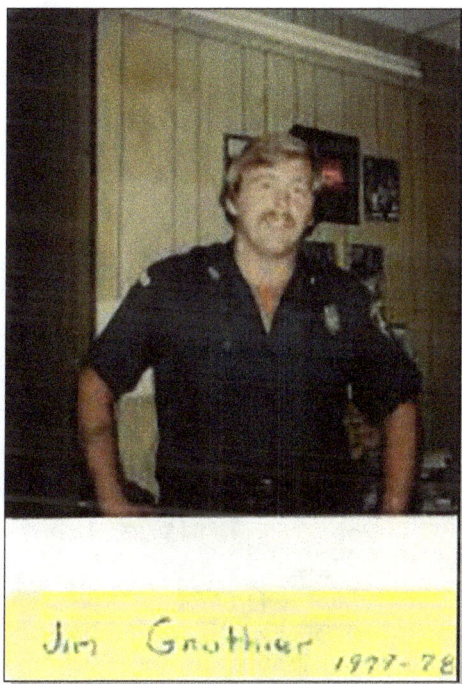

Jim Grothier 1977-78

Old 70's picture from Lena's sub shop. Courtesy of Tom Jalbert

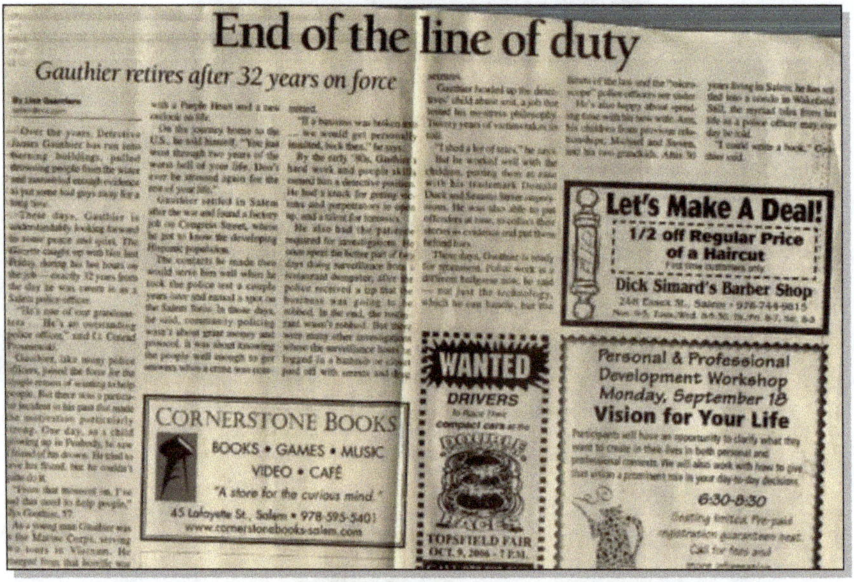

End of the line of duty

Gauthier retires after 32 years on force

CORNERSTONE BOOKS
BOOKS • GAMES • MUSIC
VIDEO • CAFÉ
"A store for the curious mind."
45 Lafayette St., Salem • 978-595-5401
www.cornerstonebooks-salem.com

WANTED
DRIVERS
TOPSFIELD FAIR

Let's Make A Deal!
1/2 off Regular Price of a Haircut
Dick Simard's Barber Shop

Personal & Professional Development Workshop
Monday, September 18
Vision for Your Life
6:30-8:30

Salem News article about my retirement in 2006

Receiving the MOVA award at the Massachusetts State House chambers form District Attorney John Blodgett

ACKNOWLEDGMENTS

This compilation of my firsthand accounts stands as a testament to the courage, resilience, and dedication of law enforcement officers who served during the decades of the 1970s, '80s, and '90s. I am deeply grateful to my former colleagues who generously allowed their names and our shared experiences to be preserved as a part of Salem's history. I must also acknowledge my family, friends, and others whose expertise was instrumental in providing the assistance needed to transfer these stories from my memory to written pages. Finally, to the readers: Your interest in the past honors the legacy of those who served back then, but also to those today. This book is dedicated to all of you, with profound appreciation for your support and interest in preserving these stories.

Old Salem Police Station on Front Street. Courtesy of
Salem Police Department's historical archives

ABOUT THE AUTHOR

James R. Gauthier, 75, is a United States Marine Corps combat veteran and Purple Heart recipient who served two tours in the Vietnam War. He then spent the next 32 years as a Salem, Massachusetts police officer (both as a Patrol Officer, and the majority of career as Detective) until his official retirement in 2006. He was awarded the "Access of Justice Award" by the Massachusetts Office of Victim's Assistance (MOVA) in 2010. Gauthier remains a forensics consultant for Salem PD to this day.

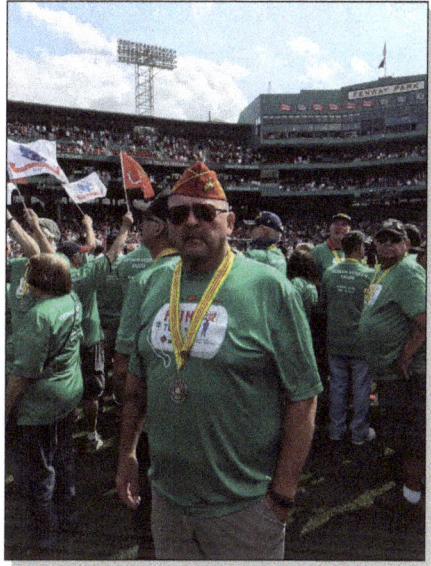

Gauthier's passion for reading history, and storytelling of the past served as the perfect combination for writing this book. He spends much of his free time today traveling with his wife Anne, exercising, spending time with his family, children, grandchildren, friends, forensics consulting, and playing the occasional round of golf.